Childhood and Adolescent Obesity

Lauren Stutts

MOMENTUM PRESS
HEALTH

MOMENTUM PRESS, LLC, NEW YORK

Childhood and Adolescent Obesity

First published in 2017 by
Momentum Press, LLC
222 East 46th Street, New York, NY 10017
www.momentumpress.net

ISBN-13: 978-1-94561-228-2 (paperback)
ISBN-13: 978-1-94561-229-9 (e-book)

Momentum Press Child Clinical Psychology "Nuts and Bolts" Collection

Cover and interior design by Exeter Premedia Services Private Ltd., Chennai, India

First edition: 2017

10 9 8 7 6 5 4 3 2 1

Printed in the United States of America.

Abstract

This book covers the development and treatment of childhood and adolescent obesity. It is written from a biopsychosocial perspective and explores obesity from a holistic perspective. First, the book addresses the extent of the obesity epidemic and how obesity is defined and assessed in children. Subsequently, it chronicles the varying causes and contributors to childhood obesity as well as the physical, psychological, and social consequences of it. Next, how childhood obesity is assessed by a psychologist and the potential psychological disorders related to obesity are discussed. The remainder of the book includes descriptions of specific interventions for childhood obesity. Moreover, the intervention section integrates a community-based perspective that is often lacking in the literature and specifically addresses underserved populations. Finally, this book concludes with practical case studies, discussion questions, and case recommendations.

Keywords

children or adolescent, health behaviors, obesity, weight loss

Contents

Acknowledgment

I would like to thank Malcolm Campbell for encouraging me to write a book and for his guidance in this process. I am also highly appreciative of Davidson College and all my mentors for supporting my academic interests.

CHAPTER 1

Description and Diagnosis

Obesity in children and adolescents is a unique and complex public health concern. Multiple global and national programs have invested significant resources into strategizing around this problem. For example, the World Health Organization has a report on recommendations to end global childhood obesity by focusing on the child's right to health, government leadership, and policies in schools, agriculture, and trade (World Health Organization 2016a). In addition, the U.S. government's program, *Healthy People 2020*, has established "children and adolescents who are considered obese" as one of their leading health foci (U.S. Department of Health and Human Services 2010). Their goal is to decrease obesity in children and adolescents from 16.9 to 14.5 percent by 2020. Another major governmental initiative that highlights the obesity epidemic is Michelle Obama's *Let's Move* campaign to reduce childhood obesity. This campaign aims to improve access to healthy foods in homes and schools, increase physical activity, and empower caregivers (White House Task Force on Childhood Obesity 2010). Clearly, the obesity epidemic has been established as a major public health concern worthy of significant time and resources. This chapter will underscore the magnitude of the obesity epidemic, how obesity is defined, and how children and parents perceive obesity.

Prevalence and Incidence of Obesity

Globally, as of 2013, there were 42 million overweight or obese young children (ages zero to five years), an increase of 10 million since 1990 (World Health Organization 2016b). The World Health Organization further notes that the increases are higher in developing countries than developed countries. Specifically in the United States, as of 2011 to 2012 around 8 percent of infants and toddlers were obese and around

17 percent of children and adolescents were obese (Ogden et al. 2014). Overall, more than one-third of children and adolescents were overweight or obese in 2012. Although obesity remains high in the United States, it appears to have reached a plateau such that the rates have stayed mostly the same in the past decade. That said, a study in 2011 indicated that the prevalence of *severe* obesity (i.e., Body Mass Index [BMI] in the 99th percentile) in children and adolescents has quadrupled since 1980 (Wang, Gortmaker, and Taveras 2011).

Significant disparities exist in the prevalence of obesity. Singh, Kogan, and van Dyck (2008) have found that children living below the poverty threshold, children who watch television greater than three hours per day, children who do not exercise at all, and children who are Hispanic and African American have significantly higher odds of being obese. Moreover, they found that children in southern states are more than twice as likely as being obese than other regions in the United States like Utah (Singh, Kogan, and van Dyck 2008). Wang, Gortmaker, and Taveras (2011) found that the prevalence of severe obesity was highest among Hispanic boys and African American adolescent girls.

Diagnosis of Obesity

Obesity is typically determined by one's BMI (Center for Disease Control 2016a). BMI is calculated by dividing one's weight in kilograms by the square height in meters. BMI is typically divided into four categories for weight: underweight, normal weight, overweight, or obese (Table 1.1). In general, having a BMI of 30 or above signifies obesity. Obesity is the term that is used clinically and by the medical profession; however, the terminology is not without its controversy (Box 1.1). There needs to be a

Table 1.1 BMI categories

BMI	Weight category	Percentile range
Below 18.5	Underweight	<5th percentile
18.5–24.9	Normal or healthy weight	5th to <85th percentile
25.0–29.9	Overweight	85th to <95th percentile
30.0 and above	Obese	≥95th percentile

Box 1.1 Is "obesity" an offensive label?

Using sensitive terminology when helping individuals is key. There are many terms that are typically not considered appropriate: fat, big-boned, person of size, well-nourished, among others. The medical profession tends to use the word "obesity"; however, that term is not without its controversy (Warin and Gunson 2013). In fact, one study found that when comparing the terms "fat" and "obese" to describe individuals, people had stronger, negative evaluations of people labeled "obese" than people labeled "fat" (Vartanian 2010). Moreover, there is a "fat acceptance" movement of individuals who are pushing back on the idea of being categorized as "obese" or as a problem to fix (Kirkland 2008). Discussion Questions: Is it acceptable to use the term "obesity"? Which label is most appropriate?

common language by which obesity is understood while still using sensitive language and not negatively labeling individuals.

Obesity in childhood and adolescence (between 2 and 18 years of age) is defined by the Center for Disease Control (2016b) as having a BMI at or above the 95th percentile for one's sex and age (Table 1.1). Being overweight is determined by being in the 85th percentile or higher, and *severe* obesity is typically defined as being in the 99th percentile or higher. For example, a 15-year-old girl who is 5'5" and weighs 160 pounds would have a BMI of 26.6, placing her in the 92nd percentile for 15-year-old girls and in the overweight category. On the other hand, a 12-year-old boy who is 5'0" and weighs 160 pounds would have a BMI of 31.2, placing him into the 99th percentile and in the obese category. Obesity in children under the age of two is measured by calculating weight and recumbent length. BMI of children and adolescents can be easily calculated online by entering age, height, and weight through the CDC website: www.cdc.gov/healthyweight/assessing/bmi/.

Although BMI is the most common and the simplest way to assess obesity, it has multiple limitations (Reilly 2010). It does not explicitly assess body fat as the "weight" includes muscle, bone, water, and body fat. Since water weight can fluctuate even within a few hours, it can influence weight by several pounds in some circumstances. Moreover, since muscle weighs more than fat, sometimes athletes have a higher BMI due to muscle weight rather than being obese. As such, there are more accurate ways of measuring body fat.

One simple way to measure problematic body fat is to measure waist circumference (Kazaks and Stern 2013). This type of measure assesses excessive abdominal fat, which is associated with the highest health risks. Although this is a helpful assessment, there is no clear evidence that it should be used to replace BMI as the main assessment of obesity in children (Reilly, Kelly, and Wilson 2010). For example, individuals sometimes have a difficult time determining what area of the abdomen is the "waist." In addition, there is no clear "normal" waist measurement by age since there is such a variation during development.

Another way that body fat is assessed is using precision calipers (Kazaks and Stern 2013). This technique is often used at health fairs because of ease of assessment. It involves measuring subcutaneous fat at the chest, hip, abdomen, thigh, or upper arm. The amount of subcutaneous fat can be used to make predictions about overall body fat. However, in children, researchers cite that measuring body fat is best assessed through a body composition analyzer rather than the calipers (Samadi et al. 2013). While measuring fat mass index is more accurate than measuring BMI in children, it requires equipment and expense.

To obtain the highest amount of accuracy in measuring body fat, higher level equipment can be used (de Vargas Zanini et al. 2015). For example, hydrostatic weighing, or weighing someone under water, allows body fat to be measured based on examining changes in density. A similar measure called Air Displacement Plethysmography (also known as the BOD POD), measures body fat based on displacement of air rather than water. There is an infant version of the BOD POD called the PEA POD for children zero to six months of age. Moreover, dual-energy X-ray absorptiometry (DXA) uses X-rays to examine energy and density of various body tissues. Although these methods are inconvenient and not generally available to use, they are highly accurate and have been successfully used to assess body fat in children (de Vargas Zanini et al. 2015).

Parent Perceptions of Weight

In order for children to be assessed in terms of their weight, parents need to regularly take them in for annual physical examinations. One problem is that parents may not perceive their child as having an unhealthy weight. When examining research on parent perceptions of weight, typically parents categorize their children in three categories (overweight, normal weight, or underweight), and their perceptions are compared to the child's actual BMI weight category. Overall, researchers have found that parents tend to underestimate children's weight, particularly when the child is overweight or obese (Parry et al. 2008; Tompkins, Seablom, and Brock 2015). However, parents do not appear to misperceive their child's weight based on their child's sex (Skinner et al. 2008).

Mareno (2014) identified five main attributes that contribute to a parent's perception of a child's weight: recognition of body size, recognition of physical appearance, recognition of functional abilities, recognition of psychosocial effects, and recognition of health effects related to current weight. One reason why misperceptions occur could be that since obesity is increasing, individuals who are obese may be seen more and more as "normal" (Mareno 2014). If the majority of one's family is overweight or one is around a community where being overweight is commonplace, then being different than overweight could be seen as less accepted. Similarly, parent preference for weight is also a consideration. For example, in some Mexican-American families, parents have expressed a preference for a child who is heavier (Pasch et al. 2016). In addition, research found that families who expressed that preference were more likely to underestimate their child's weight. The parent's weight also affects their perception of their child's weight such that overweight parents are twice as likely to underestimate their child's weight (Christofaro et al. 2016).

Regardless of the reason for the misperception, if parents do not perceive their children's weight accurately, they may be less likely to seek treatment for their children. For example, one study found that if parents underestimated their child's weight, then they were less likely to report good dietary behaviors (Skinner et al. 2008). In contrast, parents who were concerned about their child's weight made efforts such as reduced

Box 1.2 Should parents with children who are severely obese be charged with "abuse"?

In 2009 in South Carolina, Jerri Gray was charged with neglect of her 555-pound, 14-year-old son due to not taking care of him medically (Cox 2009). The Department of Social Services had intervened several times on the child's behalf, but Gray did not follow their recommendations of taking him to doctor's appointments and actively trying to help him with his weight. Gray fled SC with her son, and she was tracked down in Maryland. She was charged with a custodial interference felony and a child neglect felony. Her son was placed into foster care.

The Gray case is certainly an extreme example—her child was at risk of dying at his weight without intervention. Therefore, it would fall under the definition of child maltreatment—"any recent act, or failure to act, on the part of a parent or caretaker that results in death, serious physical or emotional harm, sexual abuse or exploitation, or an act or failure to act that presents an imminent risk of serious harm to a child" (National Institute of Justice 2016). However, what about other less extreme cases? Does the age of the child and adolescent matter?

child screen time, healthier diets, and steps to increase daily physical activity (Moore, Harris, and Bradlyn 2012). If parents are not concerned and do not make changes, then children's weight will likely continue to increase and their health could be compromised. Ultimately, those situations bring up concerns about child maltreatment (Box 1.2).

Child and Adolescent Perceptions of Weight

Children and adolescent perceptions of weight are also important to consider. Children and adolescents who are overweight have been shown to underestimate their weight compared to those who are not overweight (Maximova et al. 2008). Although both parents and adolescents tend to have misperceptions of weight, parent report is more accurate than adolescent report (Goodman, Hinden, and Khandelwal 2000). However, whereas there did not appear to be a gender difference among how parents perceived their child's weight, there appears to be a gender difference in adolescent perception. One study found that adolescent boys were more likely to underestimate weight status, and adolescent girls were more likely to overestimate weight status (Abbott et al. 2010). Similar to parents, children and adolescents were more likely to underestimate their weight when their parents and classmates were overweight (Maximova et al. 2008). Furthermore, this misperception translates to less behavioral change. For example, one study found that when adolescents underestimated their weight, they were less likely to engage in healthy dietary behaviors (Skinner et al. 2008). Overall, these results highlight the importance of accurate diagnosis and assessment in promoting intervention.

Conclusion

Clearly, childhood and adolescent obesity is a massive undertaking for public health. It is highly prevalent among most facets of society. Utilizing best practices for the diagnosis of obesity is key, and research needs to continue developing the most accurate and cost effective diagnostic tools as possible. Misperceptions among obesity status are common among parents as well as children and adolescents, and those misperceptions can lead to continued poor dietary and physical activity habits; therefore, increased exploration into the reason for those misperceptions and how to reduce them are important foci for future research as well. The next chapter focuses on the causes and consequences of obesity.

CHAPTER 2

Conceptualization

Obesity is understood to be caused by four major factors: genes, metabolism, environment, and behavior (Kazaks and Stern 2013). From a biological perspective, body fat typically increases when there is either increased energy intake or decreased energy expenditure or both. However, the process is highly complex and has significant individual variability. Ultimately, the interaction of multiple contributors is typically what leads to obesity. This chapter focuses on those major causes and addresses the multifaceted physical, cognitive, social, and psychological consequences of obesity.

Genetic Causes

Obesity is considered to be highly heritable based on twin, adoption, and family studies (Walley, Blakemore, and Froguel 2006; Yang, Kelly, and He 2007). In fact, children who have two parents who are obese have an 80 percent likelihood of becoming obese (Nguyen et al. 1996). Although heritability research is challenging since families often share genes and environments, studies examining twins who live in different families indicate that there is a stronger relationship between the twins' weight and the biological parents' weight than the adopted parents' weight (O'Rahilly and Farooqi 2008). Therefore, the genetic contribution of obesity is notable.

There are specific genetic contributions to certain forms of childhood obesity. In particular, obesity in children younger than the age of five years suggests a strong genetic cause. Some rare disorders come from single-gene mutations that lead to early-onset obesity including mutations in genes coding for leptin (*LEP*), leptin receptor (*LEPR*), propiomelanocortin (*POMC*), and melanocortin-4 receptor (*MC4R*; Yang, Kelly, and He 2007). Leptin is a hormone that helps regulate appetite;

individuals with leptin deficiencies often do not receive the clear signal to stop eating, which can lead to obesity (Cole 2007). Therefore, mutations in that gene could certainly lead to regulation problems. Having a deficiency in *POMC* is characterized by severe hyperphagia (excessive hunger) early in life (Challis and Millington 1993). *MC4R* mutations can lead to problems in the regulation of appetite and energy use (Fani et al. 2014). Moreover, childhood obesity has also been associated with the fat mass and obesity-associated gene (*FTO*) (Tovar et al. 2016). More specifically, this gene is thought to regulate eating behavior and energy expenditure (Fawcett and Barroso 2010). Studying the specific gene contributions is complex and ongoing.

Some other genetic disorders also make an individual prone to obesity. Prader–Willi Syndrome is an example of a genetic disorder associated with obesity; it results after deletion of part of Chromosome 15 and is associated with an intense interest in food (Dykens 2000). Individuals with Prader–Willi eat abnormally large amounts of food likely due to problems in the hypothalamus—a brain structure that regulates hunger and satiety. They frequently become obese as a result and develop other complications such as cardiovascular disease and diabetes mellitus (Dykens and Shah 2003). Moreover, children with developmental disabilities are more at risk for obesity than children without them (Phillips et al. 2014); this discrepancy could be due to reduced executive functioning and a less active lifestyle in some individuals with developmental disabilities.

There are also related evolutionary reasons why obesity occurs on a larger scale. In the 1960s, the idea of a "thrifty gene hypothesis" was proposed to explain that obesity occurred as a protective factor against starvation (Neel 1962). As such, it indicates that we eat in excess in case a time comes when food is not available. Moreover, living in a "food swamp," a place where unhealthy foods are more available than healthy foods, makes eating in excess commonplace. On the other hand, another theory indicates that we have a "set point" of weight that our bodies are trying to achieve (Higginson, McNamara, and Houston 2016). This theory indicates that we eat less if we start to exceed our "set point" and eat more if we go below it. These theories are challenging to study empirically, but they are certainly ideas that help us understand how obesity developed over time.

More recent research has explored the role of gut bacteria in the development of obesity (Kazaks and Stern 2013). Gut bacteria is involved with the process of using or storing calories. It is thought that individuals who are obese may have gut bacteria that are more likely to store than use calories (Cani and Delzenne 2009). Moreover, research has demonstrated that individuals who are lean have higher microbial diversity than individuals who are obese (Le Chatelier et al. 2013). Examining gut bacteria is complex because there are both genetic and environmental contributors to the composition and quantity of bacteria in the body. Further research in this area could have enormous implications on treatments for obesity.

Metabolic Causes

Another major cause of obesity is related to energy expenditure via metabolism. Metabolism encompasses the chemical reactions that occur to direct normal body functioning and consists of three main components: basal metabolic rate (60 to 70 percent), physical activity (20 to 35 percent), and the thermal effect of food (5 to 10 percent). Metabolism (i.e., basal metabolic rate) is affected by a number of factors: age, body size, stress, genetic predisposition, growth, illness, medications, sex, temperature, and time of day. Age is a particularly important consideration when studying childhood obesity. As we age, resting metabolism decreases (Luhrmann, Edelmann-Schafer, and Neuhauser-Berthold 2010). However, children typically have a high metabolism due to the growth and change in their body. As such, it is a critical time to combat weight problems because it is easier to lose weight metabolically when one is young than when one is older.

Body size is another important factor that affects metabolism. The metabolic set point was recently examined in a longitudinal study; researchers tracked 16 "The Biggest Loser" competitors over the span of six years (Fothergill et al. 2016). "The Biggest Loser" is a television show in which individuals lose massive amounts of weight within a small period of time. The researchers found that by the end of the competitors' weight loss time on the show, their metabolisms slowed radically, which made it harder to keep the weight off. Furthermore, their metabolisms stayed at that slower level even six years later, making it challenging to prevent weight gain. Thirteen out of 14 of the competitors also regained all the weight back within six years. In addition to metabolism changes, they had significantly reduced levels of leptin by the end of the show, which means that the body does not get a clear signal of satiety. While that study only included adults, it suggests that metabolism changes with body size. Similarly, however, obesity in children has also been found to negatively alter the metabolic system, though it is not completely understood how and why (Oliver et al. 2010).

In addition, thyroid impairments can lead to changes in metabolism (Rotondi et al. 2009). The thyroid gland is part of the endocrine system that helps regulate energy metabolism. Individuals with hypothyroidism have too little thyroid hormones, which can lead to weight gain. In contrast, hyperthyroidism is when the body produces too many thyroid hormones, which can lead to weight loss. While thyroid function has been studied extensively in adults, it is not as clear how it operates in children (Longhi and Radetti 2013). The relationship between the thyroid, metabolism, and body fat is highly complex, but it is generally thought that the thyroid is *not* a main cause of obesity for most individuals.

Environmental and Behavioral Causes

Outside of genetic and metabolism contributions to obesity, other major contributions are from the environment and human behaviors. These are discussed together because of how strongly the environment and behavior can affect one another. Many societies have developed into "obesogenic" environments, which is a term that indicates that high levels of unhealthy food are readily available and increased sedentary lifestyles occur in that environment to promote weight gain (Kazaks and Stern 2013). In addition, calorie consumption and portion sizes of foods have increased over time (Cohen 2014). An increase in consumption of processed, energy-dense snacks, in particular, appears to be responsible for a significant amount of that increase (Farley et al. 2010).

One of the major environments for children and adolescents is school. Unfortunately, schools frequently make unhealthy options convenient and inexpensive (Watts et al. 2015). A documentary on childhood obesity, called *Fed Up*, highlights the lack of healthy foods in schools

(Soechtig 2014). For example, they note that most public schools offer lunchtime unhealthy options daily such as cheeseburgers, nachos, French fries, and pizza. Pizza and French fries are even categorized in schools as "vegetables" as pizza contains tomato paste and fries contain potatoes. Moreover, student stores are often packed with processed foods such as chips and candy.

Children are also often targeted by mass media campaigns regarding food. Commercials during children's programming often include advertisements for sugar-sweetened beverages, fast food, and other processed, yet child-friendly food products. Children's food preferences are powerfully affected by advertising (Lioutas and Tzimitra-Kalogianni 2015), and children as young as two can even recognize brands (Soechtig 2014). Lioutas and Tzimitra-Kalogianni (2015) proposed that food advertising works in manipulating children via four routes: motivational arousal, linkage of the products related to positive feelings, linkage of entertainment of the advertising to positive feelings, and the lack of understanding over the persuasive nature of the advertising. The basic message is often that you should eat this food product to feel better, which can have a powerful negative effect on behavior. Exposure to food via advertising leads to eating more; for example, research has found that children who watch food commercials eat more food while watching television than children who are eating food and watching nonfood commercials (Soechtig 2014).

Food availability in the environment has a number of disparities. For example, children in lower socioeconomic status neighborhoods and neighborhoods that have a predominately minority population have more fast food outlets and convenience stores compared to neighborhoods with a higher socioeconomic status and of a majority population (Lee 2012). Moreover, disparities arise when considering acculturation. Several studies have indicated that individuals who immigrate to the United States and acclimate to the culture are more likely to become obese (Popkin and Udry 1998). Among Hispanic individuals, the longer time spent in the United States is related to the higher risk of obesity (Kaplan et al. 2004). The problem is thought to be particularly due to "dietary acculturation"—when individuals adopt more calorie-dense diets and consume more processed foods in cultures like the United States (Chambers, Pichardo, and Davis 2014). This type of acculturation leads to increased rates of obesity in those populations. That said, the impact of accultura-tion also depends on socioeconomic status, the availability of traditional food items, the amount of time to prepare meals, and neighborhood, among other factors.

The increasing sedentary lifestyle in children and adolescents is another contributor to obesity. Children and adolescents commonly have personal technological devices such as cell phones, iPads, and laptops, which all contribute to increased sedentary behavior. In addition, it is less acceptable for parents to let their children play outside and bike places by themselves for safety concerns (Bates and Stone 2015). Furthermore, physical education has been de-emphasized in the school curriculum, and a Harvard poll found that 7 out of 10 parents said their child does not receive any physical education (Datz 2013). High levels of seden-tary behavior do not only directly affect one's weight, but they are also related to increases in attentional and internalizing problems (Suchert, Hanewinkel, and Isensee 2015). As such, children's negative emotions could lead to increased eating and exposure to advertisements, which could further increase obesity risk.

Moreover, there are other important behavioral contributors to obe-sity. Cohen (2014) highlights three main human behavioral reasons why overeating and obesity are commonplace. First, she indicates that we have limited self-control particularly since self-control takes energy. Children, in particular have lower self-control and are less inhibited (Kopp 1982). The lower the self-control, the more likely the child is to choose unhealthy choices and eat when already full. Second, she argues that we have lim-ited cognitive capacity; for example, we often eat without thinking about how much we are eating and without thinking about how hungry or full we are. This type of behavior is particularly salient when individuals eat while engaging in another task; for example, when watching television and eating, individuals' attention is split, so overeating often goes unno-ticed. Lastly, she proposes that decisions about eating occur via automatic functioning and that our bodies or minds are easily manipulated by envi-ronmental triggers. For instance, if someone makes popcorn and we smell it, we often automatically want popcorn even if we are full.

Overall, the environment and behavioral choices are clearly import-ant contributors to the obesity epidemic in children. Many developed countries have focused more on "behavioral" reasons for obesity rather than changing the environment (Soechtig 2014; Cohen 2014). As such, there is more blame placed on individuals for being obese, and they are charged with taking personal responsibility for their weight loss. However, taking personal responsibility for weight loss has not been effective as our environment clearly makes it challenging to change unhealthy behaviors. Therefore, the focus on environmental causes and how we can create a healthier culture are key next steps.

Physical Consequences

When discussing consequences of obesity, some of the most notable and serious consequences are physical ones. For example, Reilly and colleagues (2010) highlight major physical consequences of obesity such as presence of cardiovascular and metabolic risk factors, chronic inflammation, and fatty liver, among other comorbid conditions. A particularly common condition is Type 2 diabetes mellitus (Straub 2014). With this condition, the body does not produce enough insulin, or insulin is not functioning correctly; individuals with this problem are typically referred to as having "insulin resistance." Common symptoms of Type 2 diabetes include fatigue, dryness in the mouth, numbness or pain in extremities of the body (e.g., feet and fingers), frequent urination, and slower healing of cuts. Other frequent physical comorbid conditions with obesity include: hypertension, high cholesterol, obstructive sleep apnea, arthritis, gout, and gallbladder disease (Straub 2014).

With the presence of multiple conditions, individuals then have symptoms of those conditions and need to receive treatment related to them. For example, individuals with Type 2 diabetes need to engage in regular blood glucose monitoring and give themselves insulin injections (Straub 2014). Moreover, they often need to take medications to help regulate their blood sugar such as Metformin and Prandin (Bolen et al. 2016). As such, they sometimes experience negative side effects from those medications; for example, metformin sometimes leads to muscle pain, chills, drowsiness, nausea, and diarrhea, among other unpleasant side effects. Therefore, the physical consequences of obesity are compounded by the number of comorbid conditions and the types of treatment they are receiving.

In addition, physical activity becomes more challenging when one is obese. It can be difficult for children and adolescents who are obese to keep up physically with normal-weight peers when playing sports or engaging in physical activities. Moreover, individuals who have knee or back pain when exercising will often not be able to withstand activity over a certain amount of time. One study found that children and adolescents who were obese rated higher perceived difficulty in engaging in physical activities of daily living such as walking, running, and climbing stairs compared to children and adolescents who were normal or overweight (Valerio et al. 2014). Those perceived difficulties also negatively predicted engagement in sports activities, indicating that children who struggle with activity may miss out on the physical, psychological, social, and cognitive benefits of sports participation. Additionally, this study found that children and adolescents who were obese had lower functional capacity such that they performed worse on a six-minute walking test than children who were normal or overweight.

One of the most concerning long-term physical consequences of obesity is an increased risk of obesity in adulthood, which leads to an increased risk of mortality later in life (Llewellyn et al. 2016; Reilly 2010). In addition, obesity in children is a significant predictor of other comorbid conditions in adulthood such as Type 2 diabetes in cardiovascular disease (Llewellyn et al. 2016). These dire physical consequences highlight the magnitude of the obesity problem.

Cognitive Consequences

Obesity in children is also associated with cognitive impairments. For example, a review study indicated that excess fat was related to impairments in working memory, attention, decision making, and cognitive flexibility (Liang et al. 2014). Another study found that adolescents who were obese had thinner orbitofrontal cortices than adolescents who were normal or overweight (Ross, Yau, and Convit 2015). The type of fat eaten also can result in either positive or negative cognitive effects. One study found that eating saturated fats was associated with worse relational memory (involves the hippocampus) and item memory (does not involve the hippocampus), and consumption of omega-3 fats was associated with better relational memory (Baym et al. 2014). Therefore, the hippocampus appears to be affected by the type of fat consumed.

In addition to the aforementioned effects on the brain, obesity in children is related to an impairment in inhibitory control (Reyes et al. 2015). If children struggle with inhibition, they may be more likely to eat when they are not hungry and make poorer choices about type of food when presented with unhealthy and healthy options. The combination of the brain structural differences, problems in executive functioning, and altered inhibitory control can lead other poor choices such as self-destructive behaviors and lower performance.

Social and Psychological Consequences

In addition to the physical and cognitive consequences, children and adolescents experience numerous challenges socially and psychologically as a result of obesity. Obesity is associated with high levels of stigma in the United States (Puhl and Latner 2007). Individuals who are obese are often thought of as lazy, incompetent, and with low self-control (Box 2.1). In children and adolescents, this type of thinking often leads to bullying. In fact, children who are obese are more likely to be bullied than children who are normal weight (Lumeng et al. 2010). Being bullied has negative psychological consequences. In adolescence, experiencing teasing about

Box 2.1 Do you have a weight bias?

One way to assess biases is through the Implicit Association Test (IAT) (Greenwald, McGhee, and Schwartz 1998). This type of test measures how you associate two concepts with certain attributes. For the weight IAT, it examines the association between "fat" and "thin" and the attributes of "good" and "bad." The task has to be completed quickly, so the individual does not have enough time to think about the "correct" answer. People tend to have a high antifat bias when completing this test (Wang, Brownell, and Wadden 2004). You can take the weight bias test here for free: https://implicit.harvard.edu/implicit/selectatest.html.

weight has been found to be associated with low self-esteem and higher depressive symptoms (Eisenberg, Neumark-Sztainer, and Story 2003). It is also related to increases in thinking about or attempting suicidal behaviors.

Children and adolescents who are obese are also more likely to have depression and lower quality of life than those who are not (Phillips et al. 2012). The focus on appearance and peer acceptance during development makes it challenging for someone who is obese to feel positive about themselves, which is particularly impactful for girls. For example, being obese as a female adolescent has been associated with high body dissatisfaction and low self-esteem (Wardle, Waller, and Fox 2002).

Obesity in children and adolescents also has broader social consequences. For example, it is associated with lower attainment in educational goals and socioeconomic status (Reilly 2010). Moreover, being obese in adolescence is associated with being less likely to marry and having higher rates of poverty (Gortmaker et al. 1993). Also, later in adulthood, individuals who are obese commonly experience discrimination in the workplace.

Conclusion

The main causes of obesity consist of the interaction of genes, metabolism, environment, and behavior. Therefore, some of the contributors are outside of one's control such as genes, and some are within one's control such as behavior. The environment is challenging as some aspects are within one's control and some are not. Focusing on the causes can help us figure out how to prevent and treat obesity. The negative consequences of obesity are serious and far ranging including physical, cognitive, social, and psychological sequelae. Most concerning is the likelihood of childhood obesity leading to adult obesity, which is associated with increased mortality. These consequences highlight the need for a prompt public health response to the childhood obesity epidemic. The next chapter will focus on the evaluation and assessment of psychological disorders related to obesity.

CHAPTER 3

Evaluation and Assessment

Children who are obese show greater levels of psychopathology than children who are not obese (Kalarchian and Marcus 2012). As such, children who are obese are often seen by psychologists in addition to physicians. Clinical health psychologists, in particular, are trained in helping individuals make behavior changes, such as losing weight. Moreover, individuals often use food as a coping strategy reduce negative emotions. This chapter will discuss common disorders associated with obesity including Binge Eating Disorder (BED) and Major Depressive Disorder (MDD). It will also explore intricacies of assessment of psychological disorders related to childhood obesity and include information on a specific form of assessment for prebariatric surgery.

Psychological Disorders

Binge Eating Disorder

Some individuals with obesity struggle with binge eating, which is defined by eating an atypically large amount of food within a two-hour period (American Psychiatric Association 2013). One of the other key features of binge eating is feeling like one does not have control over this behavior. Frequent and maladaptive binge eating is now referred to as a specific disorder called BED. Individuals are diagnosed if they engage in binge eating at least one time for week for three months, and the binge eating periods are associated with negative feelings and behaviors (e.g., eating until feeling uncomfortable or eating alone due to embarrassment). Within this disorder, binge eating is not accompanied by any compensatory behavior such as purging or excessive exercising or another disorder would need to be considered. It is often categorized in terms of severity ranging from mild (1 to 3 binge eating periods a week) to extreme (14 or more binge eating periods a week).

Although minimal research has specifically explored BED and children who are obese, it is thought that children are less likely to meet criteria than adults as they exhibit less frequent episodes of binge eating (Bishop-Gilyard et al. 2011). The estimated prevalence among children and adolescents is thought to be 1 to 1.5 percent (Weis 2014). However, the prevalence is particularly high among children and adolescents seeking treatment for obesity. For example, one study found that 36.5 percent of obese children and adolescents who sought care reported at least one binge eating episode per week (Decaluwé, Braet, and Fairburn 2003).

The timing of BED is also important to consider. Researchers have divided BED into two types: early-onset BED and late-onset BED (Marcus and Kalarchian 2003). Early-onset BED typically occurs around the ages of 11 and 13 years and is usually associated with weight regulation struggles in childhood. On the other hand, late-onset BED begins around 18 years of age and is typically not associated with weight regulation struggles in childhood.

Major Depressive Disorder

Depression is comorbid with obesity in childhood and adolescence (ter Bogt et al. 2006). In fact, research has also indicated that obesity is associated with having more suicidal thoughts than individuals who are not obese (van Wijnen et al. 2010). MDD is the specific diagnosis of depression (American Psychiatric Association 2013). For children and adolescents to be diagnosed with MDD, they have to present with five or more symptoms of depression over a two-week period. One of their symptoms must be either depressed mood or loss of interest in usual activities. They also must have at least four other symptoms of depression: increased or decreased appetite (often accompanied by weight gain or loss), increased or decreased amount of sleep, agitation, fatigue or loss of energy, feelings of worthlessness, difficulty concentrating, and thoughts of dying. Those symptoms also have to cause distress or impairment in the individuals' life. It is further categorized from mild to severe, depending on the number and severity of symptoms. Finally, the course of MDD needs to be differentiated as the individual may have experienced one episode of depression or recurrent episodes.

The directionality of the relationship between obesity and depression is complex, however (Weis 2014). For example, children who are depressed may be prone to eat more and use food as a coping mechanism, which could lead to overeating and obesity. On the other hand, children who are obese may experience bullying as a result of obesity and become depressed due to the indirect effects of obesity. It is most likely a bidirectional relationship, however, where obesity contributes to depression and depression contributes to obesity.

Assessment

Psychological assessment of children and adolescents who present with obesity as a problem of focus contains multiple components: clinical interview of the child and adolescent, informant interview with legal guardian, behavioral observations, and questionnaires. Prior to assessment, the psychologist often has received referral information from the child or adolescents' primary care physician. Along with this referral, it is helpful to obtain permission from the legal guardian(s) to review their medical records. This information allows the psychologist to understand the history of medical concerns as well as an objective trajectory of their weight. Moreover, medical records can give the psychologist information about the child's medication intake and any behavioral observations noted by the physician. If children and adolescents present with obesity as a problem and have not been assessed by a medical professional, then the psychologist should refer the child to one as there could be a medical reason for their obesity that needs to be ruled out first.

Clinical Interview

When interviewing a child or adolescent, the psychologist first needs to obtain permission from the legal guardian to meet with the child individually. At the beginning, the psychologist also must relay the limits of confidentiality to the legal guardian and to the child or adolescent (depending on the age of the child). Psychologists must communicate that they are bound by law to report if the child or adolescent is in imminent danger to self or others or if the psychologist suspects child abuse or neglect (Weis 2014). They also need to know that sometimes information has to be released if the psychologist receives a court order. Moreover, in order to receive payment, the psychologist often has to submit the diagnosis and treatment plan to the insurance company. However, all other information remains confidential, unless the child's parents give permission to release information to other providers.

The type and number of questions the psychologist asks children and adolescents depends on their age. If children are of elementary-school age, it is helpful to make the interview more of a "game" or as "play." For example, one technique is to tell the child that you are going to throw a ball back and forth, and when you throw the ball, you will ask a question, and when the child catches the ball, he or she answers the question, and then throws the ball back. For adolescents, however, a typical question-answer interview similar to adults works effectively.

The content of the interview will also depend on the situation. However, ideally, the psychologist would gain information from children and adolescents across a range of categories, which is summarized in Table 3.1. In the interview, it is first important to establish rapport with children, so they will be comfortable and more likely to give information. One strategy is to talk to children about something easy and fun. For example, asking children what games or sports they like to play, what they like about school, or what is their favorite color. Next, it is typically easiest to ask about physical or medical information. For example, asking children if they become ill at times, experience pain anywhere, have difficulty sleeping, or have increased or decreased appetite. From the appetite question, the psychologist will need to sensitively ask about body weight and changes. One technique to make children comfortable is to make a normalizing statement such as: "Sometimes when children eat more, they notice that their body changes. Have you noticed any changes in your body?" Other critical questions would be to ask children about how they feel about their body and what others say to them about their body (e.g., parents, friends) and how that makes them feel. From there, the psychologist should ask questions about their behavior around food or exercise. For example, "What did you have for breakfast today? What did you have for dinner last night?" Also, asking children what television shows they

Table 3.1 Assessment categories for interviews with children and adolescents who are obese (as a presenting problem)

Assessment category	Subcategory
Medical	Physical problems Pain Sleep Appetite
Weight or body or health behaviors	Weight changes Body image Messages from others about his or her body Eating behaviors Physical activity or sedentary behaviors
Psychological	Sadness (e.g., self-harm) Fear Anger Other (e.g., hearing voices) Coping strategies
Psychosocial	Family Friends School Extracurricular activities
Positive	Strengths Hope for future

watch and how often (e.g., every night, every morning) and how often they play outside or on a sports team.

After asking about their feelings about their body and their health behaviors, the psychologist needs to ask about other present feelings and history of psychological concerns (depending on age). At this point, children are likely feeling more comfortable with the psychologist, so it is easier to talk about these more challenging topics. It is important to ask about children's reports of sadness, fear, and anger, as well as how they cope with those negative emotions. Also, checking in about other symptoms like hearing voices or seeing things that aren't there is necessary for a comprehensive assessment. Asking about any self-harm or any harm of others should follow from those questions. One broad question that can help elicit answers is "Do you feel safe at home? At school?"

If not answered previously, asking children about their psychosocial history is helpful. Specifically asking them who they live with and how they feel about each person who lives with them. Next, the psychologist should ask about other support such as teachers, friends, and extended family. It can also be revealing to ask about their interest in school, what they want to be later on, their school performance, and their extracurricular interests. When wrapping up an interview, it is helpful to ask children some positive questions such as "What do you like about yourself? What are your strengths? What are you looking forward to?" to end the assessment on a positive note.

Informant Interview

After thoroughly interviewing the child or adolescent alone, the psychologist needs to interview the child's legal guardian(s) alone. The legal guardian is typically a parent. However, outside of the legal guardian, other informants could include teachers and extended family members. During your time with the legal guardian, it is important to address most of the questions that were covered with the child or adolescent and note any inconsistencies. Additional questions should be asked about the child's developmental history, obesity trends in the family, family psychiatric history, and cultural beliefs, among other historical and environmental information that children cannot readily provide. The legal guardian can usually provide more specific information and examples, which results in a more comprehensive picture.

There are several challenges to interviewing informants, however. Legal guardians may leave out or provide misleading information out of social desirability. They may also express the expectation that their child only needs to be treated or "fixed," whereas they themselves may not expect to have to makes changes. In this interview, the psychologist should emphasize the parents as important "team members" of their child's health and will be expected to make changes with their child. Another challenge is when children and adolescents do not want their parents knowing all the contents of their session with the psychologist. Since children and adolescents are minors, their parents are legally entitled to all information about their child. However, with adolescents in particular, it is wise to ask the parent if adolescent's comments can be kept private unless the parent needs to know for safety reasons. This privacy will often increase the adolescent's engagement in counseling, which can lead to better success.

Behavioral Observations

While interviewing the child or adolescent and the legal guardian, the psychologist should be observing and noting nonverbal communication and behaviors. One of the first notes to make is about their general appearance (e.g., dressed appropriately, hygiene level). Next, observing eye contact, posture, and body movements can give you helpful information. Paying attention to the speech and language can also be revealing. The attention span and length of answers is an important indicator about their functioning as well.

In addition to observing the child or adolescent and the legal guardian separately, the psychologist should note how they interact together. For example, how do they talk to one another? Do they display affection? Collecting this information will help the psychologist obtain a sense at the level of difficulty of making changes as a family. Overall, the psychologist should note inconsistencies between the interview information of the child and legal guardian and the behavioral observations. For example, if the legal guardian and the child argue and display no affection, then reports of a highly functional, positive relationship may be questioned.

Questionnaires

After the interviews, the psychologist typically chooses follow-up questionnaires based on information received in the clinical interview. For children and adolescents who are obese, there are three areas of typical questionnaires: eating behaviors, body image perceptions, and depression. Table 3.2 includes a summary of recommended measures for each category.

Eating Behaviors

To assess eating behaviors, a relevant scale is the *Children's Binge Eating Disorder Scale* (Shapiro et al. 2007). This is a 7-item questionnaire tailored for children ages 5 to 13 years that assesses yes or no responses to certain eating behaviors. For example, an example item is "Do you ever want to eat when you are not hungry?" Children are then classified as having BED

Table 3.2 **Common questionnaires for children or adolescents who are obese**

Area	Questionnaires
Eating behaviors	*Children's Binge Eating Disorder Scale* (Shapiro et al. 2007) *Questionnaire of Eating and Weight Patterns—Adolescent Version* (Johnson et al. 1999) *Children's Version of the Eating Attitudes Test* (Maloney, McGuire, and Daniels 1988)
Body image	*Body Esteem Scale* (Mendelson and White 1985) *Body Shape Questionnaire* (Cooper et al. 1987)
Depression	*Children's Depression Inventory* (Kovacs 1992) *Piers-Harris Self-Concept Scale 2* (Piers and Herzberg 2002)

if they answered yes to certain questions and reporting engaging in those behaviors for longer than three months.

The *Questionnaire of Eating and Weight Patterns—Adolescent Version (QEWP-A)* is a helpful measure for adolescents (Johnson et al. 1999). This survey has 12 questions for adolescents between the ages of 10 and 18 years. An example item is "During the past six months, did you ever eat what most people, like your friends, would think was a really big amount of food?" Most of the questions require yes or no responses. Johnson et al. (1999) also created a parent version called the *Questionnaire of Eating and Weight Patterns—Parent Version (QEWP-P)*. This survey is the same as the adolescent one, but it is tailored to the parent. An example item is "During the past six months, did your child ever eat what most people, like his or her friends, would think was a really big amount of food?" Based on an algorithm of responses, the child or adolescent is then categorized as no diagnosis, nonclinical binge eating, and BED.

A survey called the *Children's Version of the Eating Attitudes Test (ChEAT)* was created to assess feelings about eating with children ages 8 through 13 years (Maloney, McGuire, and Daniels 1988). It has 26 questions specifically about behavior and emotions connected to eating and body image. An example item is to indicate how often the child engages with this behavior: "I eat diet foods." The child ultimately receives a total score as well as a score on three subscales: dieting, restricting, and food preoccupation.

Body Image Perceptions

It is often helpful to obtain more information of how children and adolescents are feeling about their bodies. The *Body-Esteem Scale* is a common instrument used to assess how children perceive their own body (Mendelson and White 1985). This is a 20-item survey designed for children ages 7 to 12 years. An example item is "I am proud of my body." This survey was originally designed to have yes or no response pattern (Mendelson and White 1985), but it was modified by researchers into a yes, no, or sometimes, response to obtain more variability (Davison and Birch 2002). The survey results in a total body esteem score.

The original version of the *Body Shape questionnaire* (Cooper et al. 1987) assesses one's feelings about body image and shape. It has been modified from a 34-item measure to an 8-item measure (Evans and Dolan 1993). It has been used in adolescents and adults (Evans and Dolan 1993; Webb and Zimmer-Gembeck 2015). Individuals rate how frequently they have felt certain ways about their body over the past four weeks. An example item is "Have you felt ashamed of your body?" Individuals receive a total score of body dissatisfaction.

Depression

Children who are obese are more likely to experience depression than children who aren't obese (Phillips et al. 2012). Therefore, assessing for depression is critical. One of the most common questionnaires for depression in children is the *Children's Depression Inventory* (Kovacs 1992). There are several different forms of the questionnaire, but the 10-item form is often used. It is typically administered for children ages 7 to 17 years. For each item, children pick which statement of three statements reflects them the most. For example, the child could pick "I am sad once in a while," "I am sad many times," or "I am sad all the time." They subsequently obtain a total depression score.

When assessing for depression, the psychologist also needs to assess for suicidality (Weis 2014). One starting question is often "Have you ever thought about doing anything to hurt yourself?" Next, it is important to ask: "Have you ever *done* anything to hurt yourself?" Subsequently, the next question would be: "If you were to hurt yourself, what do you think you would do?" Broader questions that help obtain a sense of their current purpose and hope for the future would be to ask, "What are you living for currently? What do you hope for the future?" Based on their responses, the psychologist would develop a plan. If the child was engaging in continued harm to self or was at significant risk for harm to self, then the child should be admitted to inpatient treatment first. However, if the child has thought about it and was not engaged in current or planned action, then psychological treatment is typically given on an outpatient basis.

Another important facet of depression is feelings of worthlessness or self-esteem. Therefore, giving a measure on self-esteem is beneficial. The *Piers Harris Self-Concept Scale-2* is a common measure used to assess how children feel about themselves across six domains: Behavioral Adjustment, Intellectual and School Status, Physical Appearance and Attributes, Freedom from Anxiety, Popularity, and Happiness and Satisfaction (Piers and Herzberg 2002). It contains 60 items that children aged 7 to 18 years can complete. An example item is "I am happy the way I am." All questions are responded to with a yes or a no. Subsequently, they are given a total score and a score on each of the subscales.

Questionnaire Strengths and Limitations

The previous questionnaires are all frequently used and are relatively simple and clear to administer and score. Questionnaires allow you to obtain more information on the severity of the children's concerns as well as how they compare across a normed population. In addition, sometimes children and adolescents can be more forthcoming on a questionnaire as they are not having to speak directly to the psychologist (with the exception of the measures that are administered aloud). The aforementioned tests are reliable and valid, which increases the likelihood that the information is accurate. Moreover, questionnaires enable the psychologist to quantitatively examine change over time. For example, administering the *Children's Binge Eating Scale* before and after treatment can allow the psychologist to obtain a sense of how effective the treatment was in reducing binge eating.

The previous surveys have some notable limitations, however. Some of the children may be unaware of the answer and may simply choose a response at random. Since many of the questions require introspection, some children also may think they are being truthful but could be in denial or are responding based on what they have been told rather than how they actually feel. Moreover, some children may fear giving a "wrong" answer and choose to lie to avoid punishment. Sometimes children also can become distracted and not pay attention to the items or how they are responding. On the other hand, the questionnaires may not be as relevant for some individuals as they are for others. For example, many times testing norms are conducted on Caucasian individuals and are often gender-biased (either too many boys or too many girls in the standardized sample). Therefore, the norms may not take into account cultural differences.

Evaluation of Adolescents for Bariatric Surgery

Bariatric surgery is a treatment for severe obesity (Kazaks and Stern 2013). This treatment is becoming more of an option for adolescents today (Inge et al. 2014). To undergo bariatric surgery, the adolescent must be evaluated by a psychologist. This evaluation consists of a detailed clinical interview, informant data, and questionnaires. However, the evaluation is more complex than a typical clinical interview.

The categories covered by a bariatric surgery evaluation are summarized in Table 3.3. The psychologist first obtains current and historical information about the presenting problem. It is helpful to document the type of planned surgery as well as their self-reported height and weight. The reasons for why they want the surgery and how long they have considered it should be addressed as answers to these questions could be cause for concern. For example, if the reasons are solely around appearance or if they have only considered it for a month, then they may not truly need or be ready for the surgery.

After asking about the surgery, the psychologist should obtain a full history of their weight across development. For example, how long have they been overweight? How quickly has weight gain occurred (e.g., steady increase, sudden increase, increase or decrease cycle)? Next, the

Table 3.3 Assessment categories for interviews with adolescents being considered for bariatric surgery

Assessment category	Subcategory
Surgery	Type of surgery or physician Current self-reported height or weight Reasons for bariatric surgery Length of time considering bariatric surgery
Weight	Length of time with weight concerns Speed of weight changes Why have weight concerns How has weight interfered with life What weight loss strategies have been tried Records of amount and length of weight loss success Eating disorder history
Health behaviors	Typical eating patterns Typical drinking patterns Physical activity or exercise
Preparedness	Sources of information Nutritional requirements or restrictions Risks Social support Obstacles Implementation of changes Expectations or goals of weight loss postsurgery
Psychological functioning	Current psychological functioning History of psychological functioning Use of psychotropic medications Use of counseling Coping strategies
Medical or substance use or history	Medical disorders Pain or headaches Sleep or appetite Alcohol use Nicotine use Recreational drug use Other medications
Psychosocial history	Living situation Immediate family information Friends information Educational background Vocational background (if applicable) Extracurricular activities

psychologist should ask why they think they have had difficulty managing their weight (e.g., genetics, sedentary job) and specifically how their weight has impacted their life. It is critical to note what they have tried to lose weight as well as if they have been successful previously. Specifically, the psychologist should ask if they have tried any of the following: diets, exercise, laxatives, vomiting, and food restriction. From those questions, it is important to assess eating disorder history. The psychologist should subsequently ask about "a day in the life" of eating, drinking, and exercise. Often, it is simplest to ask them about those activities based on the day prior to the evaluation, so the information is more easily accessible.

Next, the psychologist should inquire about preparedness for the surgery. For example, how did they learn about the surgery? It is also important to obtain a sense of their understanding of the lifestyle changes they will have to make. What is their sense of the nutritional requirements and restrictions? Do they understand the risks of undergoing the procedure? Bariatric surgery requires support from the family, so it is helpful to learn what kind of assistance they will have. Asking them what any obstacles are (e.g., eating smaller portions) for them specifically and how they plan to address them. It is typically recommended that individuals go ahead and begin to make some of the changes before the surgery, so the changes will not be such of a shock. Therefore, the psychologist should ask them if they have started making changes. Lastly, obtaining a sense of their expectations postsurgery is revealing. For example, if they expect to go from 350 to 110 pounds in a year, then that would not be a realistic expectation.

Subsequently, the psychologist should obtain detailed information about their current psychological functioning. Individuals are sometimes wary of being forthcoming about their psychological functioning for fear that it will preclude them from the surgery. However, it typically does not interfere with that recommendation if they are taking care of themselves and aware of the resources available to them. Some important questions include asking about what kinds of stressors do they have and how stress affects them. Any current symptoms of depression, anxiety, or anger? Asking about any previous disorders as well is critical. The psychologist needs to obtain a sense of the psychological treatment they currently receive or have received in the past. Have they taken psychotropic medications or attended counseling?

After obtaining psychological information, it is important to ask about other medical problems they are experiencing as well. For example, do they have cardiovascular disease? In addition, do they experience headaches or pain in any part of their body? Following from those questions, the psychologist should ask about sleep and appetite changes and any medications they are taking. For example, if they take regular narcotics for pain management, then it could be concern.

Bariatric surgery is often easier if individuals have social support. Therefore, the psychologist should ask about their living situation and who will be available to help them. On that note, if there are any toxic friends or family that could interfere with their lifestyle changes, then that is critical to consider. Aside from family influences, the psychologist should ask about their school situation and how they spend their time outside of school. Adolescents are often influenced by their peers, so if their peers overeat frequently and they join in, then that could put them at risk for health complications.

After conducting the thorough clinical interview as aforementioned, the psychologist should see if the information is corroborated by the legal guardian. The legal guardians especially need to be aware of the lifestyle changes their child will need to make and the risks of the procedure. Coupling that information with adolescent responses to questionnaires gives a more holistic picture of the adolescent's situation. Price et al. (2015) recommend giving the adolescent the *Minnesota Multiphasic Personality Inventory-Adolescent version (MMPI-A)* and the *Family Adaptability and Cohesion Scale-IV (FACES-IV)*. The *MMPI-A* is a 478-item measure that assesses personality traits and psychopathology in adolescents aged 14 to 18 (Butcher et al. 1992). It includes 10 clinical scales: hypochondriasis, depression, hysteria, psychopathic deviate, masculinity-femininity, paranoia, psychasthenia, schizophrenia, hypomania, and social introversion. On the other hand, the *FACES-IV* is designed to assess family cohesion and flexibility (Olson 2008). It contains 42 items across six scales: balanced cohesion, balanced flexibility, disengaged, enmeshed, rigid, and chaotic. Individuals rate how much the items represent their family. An example item is "Family members are involved in each others' lives."

Individuals receive total scores on each of the six scales. The combination of these measures can help the psychologist obtain a sense of any personality, emotional, and family barriers.

Ethical Considerations

Price et al. (2015) highlighted several ethical considerations for adolescent bariatric surgery. They indicated that legally, there has to be consent from the legal guardian and assent from the adolescent. For example, if the parent consents for their adolescent to undergo the surgery, but the adolescent does not want the surgery, then the surgery should not be performed.

Another consideration is the risk versus benefit of undergoing the surgery (Price et al. 2015). If the adolescent's health is severely compromised due to having multiple comorbid conditions related to obesity, then the benefits of undergoing the surgery likely outweigh the risks. On the other hand, if an adolescent only has one or two comorbidities and is physically able to exercise, then surgery may not be worth the risk. Finally, the ability for the adolescent to make lifestyle changes should be considered. Bariatric surgery has significant nutritional and behavioral restrictions; therefore, the adolescent and family must be prepared to make those changes and adhere to them.

Overall, an entire team needs to come together to address the earlier concerns and work with the family to find the optimal treatment plan. One mandatory rule that helps with this decision is that there is a required six-month preoperative program that adolescents and their families must complete to even be considered for surgery (Cohen and Datto 2015). This thorough process prevents individuals from jumping into a surgery without being prepared or without thinking through the decision.

Conclusion

Clearly, assessment of children and adolescents who are obese as a presenting problem needs to be comprehensive. The psychologist needs to integrate all information from the clinical interview with child and adolescent, interview with legal guardian, behavioral observation notes, and questionnaire data. Ideally, these facets of information would converge to support a clear diagnosis and treatment plan. However, inconsistencies between those measures highlight a need for more information. It is also important to note that sometimes clear diagnoses do not arise. Children and adolescents may not meet criteria for any psychological disorder and simply need help managing their weight.

If children and adolescents have a clear diagnosis, then it does not necessarily need to be shared with them. At the end of the assessment, a more pragmatic approach would be to establish goals and a treatment plan. It is usually not recommended that "weight" goals are established (e.g., child and adolescent will lose 30 pounds). Since the child and adolescents' weight will be increasing anyway due to growth, it is not the best indicator of success. Instead, establishing behavioral goals are more appropriate. For example, goals might be to exercise for one hour a day, eat five servings of vegetables a day, reduce binge eating from seven times a week to one time a week, and only have two desserts a week. The psychologist would work with the child and adolescent and the family to establish the goals and proceed with a treatment plan. Specific information about treatment options are discussed in the next chapter.

CHAPTER 4

Treatment and Intervention

After a comprehensive evaluation and the creation of goals as discussed in Chapter 3, treatments centered around improving health behaviors need to be chosen. There is no one recommended treatment for obesity for children and adolescents. Treatment recommendations should be based on age, level of severity of obesity, family characteristics, resources, and individual preferences, among other factors. For example, a young child would not be recommended for cognitive-behavioral therapy due to the cognitive demands, and adolescents with less severe levels of obesity would not be recommended for bariatric surgery. That said, treatments should generally be based off of making lifestyle changes rather than strict diets and should encourage body positivity rather than body shaming. This chapter explores effective techniques for behavior modification overall as well as specific dietary and physical activity recommendations. It also addresses the possibility of pharmacological and surgical interventions. Treatments for individuals with comorbid psychological disorders are discussed next. Lastly, this chapter includes sections on interventions targeted toward underserved populations as well as broader community interventions.

Overall Behavioral Modification

Basic behavioral modification techniques are important to describe first when working with individuals for behavior change. Often individuals have developed maladaptive habits over time, which need to be altered. There are four major categories of behavior change techniques that are highly relevant to weight loss in children and adolescents: stages of change or motivational interviewing, operant conditioning, social learning or modeling, and stimulus control.

First, in changing health behaviors, the stages of change model and motivational interviewing are commonly used (Kazaks and Stern 2013). These techniques are particularly appropriate for adolescents who are obese and parents of children who are obese. The stages of change model entail categorizing people into one of six stages of readiness to change (Prochaska et al. 1994):

1. Precontemplation: The individual is not ready to change.
2. Contemplation: The individual is considering change.
3. Preparation: The individual is planning for change.
4. Action: The individual is changing.
5. Maintenance: The individual continues the behavior change.
6. Relapse: The individual reverts back to previous behavior before the change.

It is helpful to find out what stage of change adolescents are at in order to determine how ready they are to engage in a treatment plan. Regardless of the stage of change, however, the psychologist can work with them to move them to the next stage through a technique called motivational interviewing.

Motivational interviewing is a client-centered counseling technique that is designed to help individuals make behavior changes by resolving ambivalence and creating specific goals (Miller and Rollnick 1991). For example, if adolescents are at the precontemplation stage, the psychologist can work with them to identify values and how current behavior contrasts with those values. If adolescents indicate that health and appearance are important values, yet note that their behavior does not reflect those values, then this discrepancy can help them to consider the need for change. Similarly for parents of children who are obese, it is often the parents that need to make the behavior change to help their children. For example, if parents take their children out to eat fast food four times per week, then the parents are the ones who will need to engage in behavior change. If parents are not ready to make changes, then it can be a significant barrier to working with their children to help them lose weight.

Since younger children are less cognitively ready for motivational interviewing, other behavior modification techniques can be used. Operant conditioning, in particular, is effective in changing behavior (Weis 2014). Operant conditioning consists of whether a stimulus is applied or removed and how that either increases or decreases behavior. Table 4.1 highlights the four categories of operant conditioning. Behavior change is more effective when using reinforcement. Therefore, parents would be encouraged to give rewards for healthy behaviors. For example, children who exercise for an hour would be allowed to pick out a small toy from the store. Another technique is to give children tokens or stickers for each day that they complete the desired behavior and then they earn a bigger prize if they complete the desired behaviors everyday that week. For instance, if children eat two servings of vegetables everyday that week, then they earn a trip to an amusement park. It is important, however, that food and sedentary behavior are not used as reinforcement. It would not be helpful to reinforce eating vegetables, for example, with ice cream or watching television. Therefore, reinforcing with an activity or an object is more appropriate. Although reinforcement is ideal, at times punishment will need to be used. For example, if children sneak candy, then a negative punishment could be executed such that they have to go to time-out.

Another behavior change technique is called social learning or modeling (Weis 2014). Children learn behaviors by watching what others do. Parents and siblings, in particular, can be powerful models. Parents can model exercise by exercising daily, requiring children to be part of a regular sport, and making family activities related to exercise (e.g., family hikes, pool time). Moreover, exposing children to role models who exercise can be helpful. For example, having children learn about athletes like gymnast Gabrielle Douglas, basketball player Stephan Curry, football

Table 4.1 The four categories of operant conditioning

	Stimulus applied	**Stimulus removed**
Behavior increases	Positive reinforcement	Negative reinforcement
Behavior decreases	Positive punishment	Negative punishment

player Peyton Manning, and paralympic athlete Amy Purdy could inspire more activity.

Stimulus control is an additional behavior modification technique that is effective in weight loss (Kazaks and Stern 2013). Parents of children and adolescents need to be particularly aware of stimulus control. Behavior is often strong due to habits and associations; stimulus control allows individuals to capitalize on that relationship to increase the likelihood for success. For example, if individuals eat at the same time and place daily, then it decreases the likelihood of eating outside that time. In addition, by storing food out of sight, food is less likely to come to mind and less likely to be eaten impulsively. Putting exercise equipment in high traffic areas and putting equipment related to sedentary behaviors out of reach can also increase physical activity. For example, putting the remote control and other technological devices (e.g., laptop, iPad) in hard-to-reach places can reduce their use and likely result in a more mobile replacement activity.

Dietary Intervention

Dietary interventions related to nutrition and eating behavior are key components of weight loss treatment (Kazaks and Stern 2013; Straub 2014). One of the first dietary-related techniques that is used is called self-monitoring. This technique includes recording all food intakes for one week in a "food diary" or through a food-related application before treatment begins to obtain a sense of the current eating or drinking habits. Individuals typically record what they eat or drink right after they are consumed. This baseline diary can help establish average calorie intake per day, how much protein is consumed, how many servings of fruits or vegetables, and how much sugar is consumed, among other observations. Research has shown that individuals tend to underestimate food consumption (Subar et al. 2003); therefore, simply engaging in this exercise can help individuals obtain a more accurate picture of consumption. Adolescents could utilize self-monitoring, but parents should record the food diary for younger children. One excellent free phone application is called "My Fitness Pal." Food products can be scanned in or entered, and information is saved for frequently consumed foods. It also can produce summary information that is helpful for the user. One alternative way to obtain food information, particularly at restaurants where nutritional information is not readily available, is to take pictures of what is consumed.

After baseline self-monitoring, it is helpful to establish daily goals for the child or adolescent. For example, there may be a daily goal of eating three servings of vegetables. With adults, there is often a daily calorie goal that is not to be exceeded. However, with children and adolescents, it is a bit more complex as calorie needs change during development. Baylor College of Medicine has a free calculator that determines daily calorie intake based on the child's sex, age, height, weight, Body Mass Index (BMI), and activity level: www.bcm.edu/cnrc-apps/bodycomp/energy/energyneeds_calculator.htm. The National Institutes of Health also has a general summary sheet of calorie needs by sex, age, and activity level: www.nhlbi.nih.gov/health/educational/wecan/downloads/calreqtips.pdf. Subsequently, calorie goals could be calculated. To lose weight, children and adolescents need to consume less calories that their daily requirements to have a calorie deficit. However, since calorie needs increase as a child ages, it is likely a better approach to focus on eating healthier foods at the right serving size each day rather than having children and adolescents monitor calorie intake.

Another important part of dietary interventions is nutrition education. The United States Department of Agriculture has an excellent website called "Choose My Plate": www.choosemyplate.gov. It clearly highlights how foods in a meal should be distributed; at least half of the child's meal should be fruits and vegetables (Figure 4.1). The concept of serving size is another important topic to teach children and adolescents. Research has shown that as portion size increases, consumption increases in children; therefore, distributing the right portion size during mealtime is critical (Savage et al. 2012). Children and adolescents can also be taught how to identify serving sizes, which are clearly labeled on nutrition labels. Parents can make a game out of teaching children about nutrition by having them learn serving sizes and then "guessing" serving sizes. For example, showing children what one serving of cereal looks like (usually a cup) and then having children pour it themselves and whoever gets closest to a cup wins a prize.

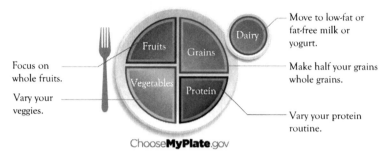

Figure 4.1 ChooseMyPlate figure

Note: This figure is in the public domain.

Many adult dietary interventions involve specific diets such as Weight Watchers or the Mediterranean diet. However, it can be dangerous for children and adolescents to go on specific diets because they often are too restrictive and too challenging to follow. In fact, there was significant controversy over a mother who wrote a book about putting her child on a diet (Box 4.1). Therefore, a better approach is to instead make lifestyle dietary changes. For example, for a lunch meal, having children and adolescents choose a vegetable, a fruit, a grain, a protein, and a dairy product. Giving around three choices for each can allow the child to feel more autonomous. Child-friendly foods in each category are shown in Table 4.2. Making foods in unique shapes and sizes can help make eating healthy food fun. Letting the children help make the food also can increase the likelihood of them eating it; therefore, children should be given small jobs to complete for each meal.

In addition to eating healthy foods, only allowing children to eat unhealthy food as a special occasion is a helpful technique. It is recommended that unhealthy foods are not kept in the house and are only eaten at times when the family leaves the house. For example, instead of providing ice cream for dessert everyday, parents can give children a Greek Yogurt popsicle as a dessert at home and have ice cream once a month only when the family goes out specifically for ice cream. Establishing rules about sugar-sweetened beverage intake is also important. Parents should provide water as the main drink at home and refrain from giving the child soda, juice boxes, or other sugar-sweetened beverages. This strategy

Box 4.1 Should parents put their children who are obese on a diet?

Dara-Lynn Weiss is a mother with a child who was obese. She wrote a book called "The Heavy" that detailed her experience with helping her seven-year-old child lose weight (Weiss 2013). There was online backlash about her regulation of her child's food intake; for example, her child was not allowed to eat the same meals as her siblings, was not allowed to eat freely at other children's houses, and was given Diet Coke to drink. That said, this book highlights the complexities of treating childhood obesity. Where is the line between helping children be healthier and "fat-shaming?" How many restrictions are too many restrictions?

Table 4.2 Examples of healthy foods per categories

Vegetables	Fruits	Grains	Protein and dairy
Zucchini "fries"	Apple	Wheat wrap	Turkey
"Spaghetti" squash	Grapes	Wheat pita	Grilled chicken
Cauliflower "popcorn"	Orange	Popcorn	Salmon
Celery	Strawberries	Brown rice	Mackerel
Spinach	Avocado	Oatmeal	Greek yogurt
Carrots	Blueberries	Quinoa	Milk

emphasizes that high fat, high sugar foods, and sugar-sweetened beverages should be eaten in moderation.

Another important component of dietary interventions is teaching children and adolescents how to eat. First, children and adolescents need to think about their hunger and satiety signals. One way to assess feelings of hunger or satiety is to rate them on a scale from 1 (starving) to 10 (uncomfortably full). Children and adolescents should eat when they feel they are around a Number 3 and stop eating around a Number 7 when beginning to feel full. When children are hungry during non-meal times, parents can provide "free snacks" that are low calorie such as carrots, celery, watermelon, or oranges. Children and adolescents would also benefit from learning how to eat mindfully. Mindful eating includes paying close attention while eating and not engaging in other activities

(Kristeller and Wolever 2014). For example, not allowing children to eat while watching television, reading, or being on the computer. Based on previous research with adults, it is likely that children will eat less when eating mindfully (Kristeller and Wolever 2014).

An example of a formal weight loss system developed for children is called the "Traffic Light" system. It entails categorizing foods into three domains: green, yellow, and red. Green foods are foods that are high in nutrients and low in energy such as spinach, celery, and carrots. Yellow foods tend to have moderate nutrients and moderate energy such as cereal, bread, and fruit. Red foods are low in nutrients and high in energy such as cake, ice cream, and fried food. Children are encouraged to eat mostly green foods (green as in "go"), some yellow foods (yellow as in "slow down"), and minimal red foods (red as in "stop"). This system is fun and simple for children to follow. Using this system in concert with physical activity has been shown to reduce BMI in children (Epstein et al. 2008).

Physical Activity Interventions

In addition to reducing energy intake, it is important to increase energy expenditure through physical activity and exercise. The term "physical activity" is a broad term used to describe movements related to activities of daily living (e.g., washing dishes), whereas "exercise" is purposeful physical activity (e.g., playing volleyball) (Kazaks and Stern 2013). The Center for Disease Control recommends that children exercise for at least an hour a day (Center for Disease Control 2016c). There are three types of physical activity children should engage in at least three times per week: aerobic activity, muscle strengthening, and bone strengthening. Aerobic activity is often divided up into moderate-intensity (e.g., walking) and vigorous-intensity (e.g., running). Muscle strengthening can occur when a child is on the monkey bars or does pushups, and jumping rope is an excellent bone-strengthening exercise. Additional examples of physical activity ideas for children and adolescents are shown in Table 4.3.

Children and adolescents are not getting the amount of exercise they need (Center for Disease Control 2016e). The Hierarchy of Walking Needs was created to explain why it is difficult for many children and their families

Table 4.3 Examples of exercise by category for children and adolescents

	Children and adolescents
Moderate-intensity aerobic activity	Rollerblading/biking Fast walking Canoeing Skateboarding Baseball Dodgeball Hiking Red rover Walk the dog
Vigorous-intensity aerobic activity	Swimming Running Soccer Basketball Tag Obstacle courses
Muscle strengthening exercises	Tug-of-war Rock climbing Monkey bars Crunches Pull-ups
Bone strengthening exercises	Jumping rope Running Gymnastics Tennis Hop-scotch

to obtain their exercise needs (Alfonzo 2005). This model indicates that exercise must first be feasible, then accessible, then safe, then comfortable, and finally pleasurable. If exercise is not safe (e.g., dangerous neighborhood), then the individual will likely choose not to exercise. Research has found that accessibility of exercise in children is associated with a lower risk of being obese (Taylor et al. 2014). Therefore, these different barriers in a child's family will need to be assessed and tackled. For example, if children are in unsafe neighborhoods such that they cannot go outside to walk, then they can follow fun video exercises online inside (e.g., videos on YouTube called "Instant Recess" can be followed along to the steps). In fact, Internet-based physical activity interventions have also been shown to be successful in increasing exercise (Müller and Khoo 2016).

One popular way to monitor and increase physical activity is through the use of pedometers. Research has indicated that using pedometers can help increase awareness of a child's physical activity as early as age three years (Robinson and Wadsworth 2010). It is recommended that girls between the ages of 6 and 12 years obtain around 12,000 steps per day and boys obtain around 15,000 per day (Tudor-Locke et al. 2004). These guidelines eventually average around 10,000 recommended steps for adolescents and adults. Parents can make increasing steps fun by making contests in the family such that whoever walks the most steps wins a prize. Moreover, parents can encourage the use of fun phone applications that encourage increased exercise such as Pokemon Go.

One way to ensure children and adolescents will get sufficient exercise is if they are on a sports team or involved in a structured exercise class (e.g., dance). Parents can indicate that all family members (including parents) must engage in regular exercise. Requiring children to always have a team sport or group (e.g., dancing) is a great strategy to make sure they are regularly active and receiving coaching for safe movements. It does not matter what sport it is, though, so allowing children a sense of control by getting to choose the sport can increase the likelihood that children will be cooperative. A team sport, in particular, allows children and adolescents to not think about it as exercise, helps them form social skills, often has reinforcement such as winning games, and allows them to receive coaching for improved performance, among other benefits.

Another way to increase physical activity is to engage in it as a family. Research has shown that family physical activity interventions can effectively increase physical activity and promote long-term change in the family (Van Allen et al. 2015). For example, the family can go on a hike up a mountain, take pictures of wildlife, and enjoy being in nature while exercising. Parents can also require children to complete chores at home that not only teaches them skills and taking responsibility, but it also adds more physical activity to their day.

Pharmacological and Surgical Interventions

Pharmacotherapy and surgical interventions should be used with caution in children and adolescents. The prefrontal cortex (e.g., planning, decision making, personality) part of the brain does not fully develop until individuals are in their mid-20s (Weis 2014); therefore, adding foreign chemicals to the brain could alter its development. There are also countless scams about "magic" weight loss drugs that actually have neither been studied scientifically nor been passed by the Food and Drug Administration (FDA). Parents should research any diet supplement thoroughly and talk with their physician about it before giving it to children.

That said, Orlistat, a lipase inhibitor, was the first FDA-approved drug for the treatment of obesity in children ages 12 years and older (Chanoine and Richard 2011). It is designed to prevent absorption of all ingested fat. It has been shown to increase weight loss and is safe to use for up to one year. However, it is associated with unpleasant side effects such as liquid stools, fecal urgency, flatulence, and stomach cramping (Kazaks and Stern 2013). While this medication can be effective, it should only be used if recommended by a physician and if many other behavioral weight loss strategies have not worked.

Bariatric surgery is another option that should be used with caution. It is becoming more of a common treatment for adolescents, as discussed in Chapter 3 (Inge et al. 2014); however, it should only be considered when an adolescent has high-risk obesity with multiple comorbidities, is unable to exercise, and when multiple previous treatments have been unsuccessful. It is typically used as a last resort for extreme cases. There are several types of bariatric surgeries, but the most common types in adolescents are the Roux-en Y gastric bypass (RYGB) and the laparoscopic gastric banding (LAGB) (Inge et al. 2014). Both surgeries result in restricting how much food the stomach can hold, which typically results in a faster feeling of satiety and reduced food intake. Undergoing the surgery has been associated with weight loss, reduced depression, and increased quality of life (Hillstrom and Graves 2015).

While bariatric surgery can be effective, it comes with many risks. For example, the individual could die during the surgery, experience gastrointestinal leakage, bowel obstructions, infections, and bleeding (Kazaks and Stern 2013). Nutritional deficiencies can also occur when individuals do not take care of themselves. Moreover, it results in life-long lifestyle changes that can be challenging to follow, particularly for an adolescent. Individuals are advised to eat several small meals a day, with each meal being only about a half a cup of food at a time. They have to increase the amount of protein and decrease the amount of carbohydrates. They also have to eliminate caffeinated beverages, carbonated beverages, and alcohol from their diet. These are just several of the major daily changes adolescents would need to follow for the rest of their life. Therefore, a comprehensive evaluation from an interdisciplinary team should determine the costs and benefits of recommending or not recommending bariatric surgery for adolescents.

Interventions for Comorbid Psychological Disorders with Obesity

Binge Eating Disorder

Cognitive-behavioral therapy (CBT) is the most common treatment used for Binge Eating Disorder in adolescents (Vocks et al. 2010). It is based on the assumption that thoughts influence feelings, which influence behavior. First, the psychologist helps individuals recognize thoughts and feelings that precede a binge episode (Weis 2014). The psychologist teaches individuals to reduce negative feelings through healthy coping strategies that do not involve food. For example, if adolescents are stressed, instead of eating, then they would call a friend or go outside for a walk. Other sessions entail identifying and challenging automatic thoughts and cognitive distortions related to eating. A common distortion is "I can't stop eating." The psychologist would then work through a thought record to help the individual evaluate the validity of that thought and come up with an alternative, more accurate thought. Parents are often included in CBT as well to make sure they help their children and adolescents work on altering their thoughts and behaviors. CBT has overall been shown to be more effective than medication alone or a weight-loss program alone in reducing binge eating in adolescents (Vocks et al. 2010).

Another treatment that has been used to reduce binge eating is called Interpersonal Therapy (IPT). This type of therapy addresses interpersonal conflict and stress that relates to maladaptive behaviors (Markowitz and Weissman 2012). It has been successfully adapted to treat Binge Eating Disorders (Wilfley et al. 1998). Adolescents may have conflict with friends, which can lead to depression and maladaptive coping skills such as binge eating. Binge eating could also be related to other interpersonal problems such as parental divorce, parental illness or death, and role transitions. Through this therapy, adolescents are taught communication skills, conflict resolution skills, and how to cope with interpersonal stress. Research has found that IPT is a highly effective treatment for Binge Eating Disorder, and it has been shown to be more effective than behavioral weight loss programs (Hilbert et al. 2015).

Major Depressive Disorder

Similar to Binge Eating Disorder, CBT is the first line of treatment for Major Depressive Disorder (Weis 2014). Since depression can both be a contributor and a consequence to obesity, then it is important to evaluate thoughts related to self-esteem as well as thoughts that surround negative feelings related to eating behaviors. Often individuals who are obese overemphasize the importance of weight and its reflection of them as a person; therefore, the psychologist would help them change those cognitive distortions and accept themselves. Sometimes by helping individuals increase their self-esteem, they are more prone to engage in self-care behaviors such as eating healthier and exercising because they feel they are worth it. If children and adolescents are severely depressed and are at risk for harming themselves, then they should be placed in inpatient psychiatry for more ongoing intensive treatment.

Interventions for Underserved Populations

While the preceding interventions can be used effectively, there are some underserved populations that do not have access to them. Therefore, interventions for underserved populations need to be completed in collaboration with the communities themselves. For example, leaders in the community should be included in the planning and decision making as they most closely understand the needs of their individual community.

One underserved population for obesity interventions in the United States is the Latino community (Ramirez, Gallion, and Despres 2014). Some barriers have included the following: both parents having demanding work schedules, lack of emphasis in the family on physical activity, and neighborhood safety concerns. Including *promotoras*, individuals from the community who receive training on disseminating basic health education, and *cuaranderos*, community health care workers whose focus is on alternative treatments, in the conversation can help find ways to realistically and sensitively address those barriers. One study called the Healthier Options for Public Schoolchildren (HOPS) employed a holistic school-based intervention program that taught children in a Hispanic community about adapted food choices, lifestyle education, physical activity, and overall wellness projects (Hollar et al. 2010). After the study, children had reductions in BMI, blood pressure, and improvements in academic scores. Another study found longitudinal outcomes in using an intensive lifestyle-based weight maintenance program for children who are Mexican-American; reductions in weight and improvements in clinical factors (e.g., reductions in cholesterol) were maintained two years after the intervention (Johnston et al. 2010).

Another underserved population is the African-American community (Beech and Jernigan 2014). There is evidence that African-American girls have a particularly difficult time maintaining weight due to reduced fat oxidation rates and reduced resting metabolic rates compared to other ethnic groups (White and Jago 2012). Effective interventions have mostly been conducted in community settings with a focus on dance as the physical activity of choice (Beech and Jernigan 2014). Another helpful strategy is using an after-school girls' club to promote the intervention (Story et al. 2003).

Other communities that often receive fewer services are rural communities (Greening et al. 2011). One study creatively examined the use of training adolescent students to learn about healthy lifestyle changes and serve as leaders to enact community change (Branch et al. 2014). Moreover, due to the geographic barriers, using telemedicine to ask questions and provide health education is a way to connect more frequently with individuals and communities (Shaikh, Nettiksimmons, and Romano 2011).

Community Interventions

Some neighborhoods are built within an obesogenic environment characterized by high access to unhealthy foods and minimal access to healthy foods (Straub 2014). One intervention is to increase the community access to a farmer's market or create a community garden. Another strategy is to organize a "town 5k" where community members are encouraged to train for and complete a 5k to raise money for a community need. Employing programs that encourage breast-feeding and increased maternal care in the workplace can also make an impact.

There are multiple national public health programs designed to reduce the obesity epidemic. One is Michelle Obama's *Let's Move* initiative to increase healthy eating and physical activity in children and families. One unique aspect of this program is the "Chefs Move to Schools" program, which is designed to teach culinary skills to children in schools. However, this program is not formally evaluated, so its effectiveness is unclear. *Healthy People 2020* is a broader initiative conducted by the U.S. Department of Health and Human Services to reduce disease and improve quality of life of Americans. This initiative is evaluated formally and is currently in progress.

On a broader scale, changing governmental policies and the broader food environment is an area of intervention (Kazaks and Stern 2013). The Center for Disease Control (CDC) has recommended a holistic MAPPS (media, access, point-of-purchase, price, and social and support services) program for community changes (Center for Disease Control 2016d). The first component of the MAPPS program is the media—its focus is to improve the media's exposure of healthy foods and physical activity and limit advertising for unhealthy foods. Access is the second component and is based on increasing availability of healthy grocery stores, reducing density of unhealthy food establishments, and enhancing neighborhood and park safety to increase physical activity. The third component is the point-of-purchase promotion; it involves improving menu and nutritional labeling and increasing signage for healthy options and walkable areas. Price is the fourth component and is related to making healthy food affordable and giving incentives for active mobility. Lastly, social and support services are related to increasing healthy options in public settings such as sports events and promoting community physical activity groups. These collective efforts can make it easier for individuals to develop healthier behaviors.

More controversial larger-scale proposals are the use of increasing taxes on unhealthy foods and the increased regulation of the food industry. Increasing taxes for sugar-sweetened beverages, in particular, has been suggested since increases in taxes for cigarettes and alcohol have been successful in reducing consumption of those products (Fletcher, Frisvold, and Tefft 2011). However, the regulation of sugar is more complicated, and research suggests that it may not have as strong as an impact as it did with cigarettes and alcohol (Powell and Chaloupka 2009).

The regulation of the industry is another difficult intervention to tackle. In her book *My Big Fat Crisis*, Cohen recommends having density restrictions on number of unhealthy restaurants in an area, standardizing portion sizes across restaurants, employing restrictions of impulse marketing (no candy at the registers), requiring counter-advertising (for every unhealthy food ad, include a healthy food ad), and improved warning labels on unhealthy foods, among others (Cohen 2014). The documentary, *Fed Up*, also makes strong arguments for the need for increased regulation. It particularly emphasizes the need to separate the relationship between schools and companies such as Coca-Cola, Pepsi, and Dominos to make their products unavailable to students at school. While the specifics of changes that need to be made are likely multifaceted, it is clear that some major changes in the food industry need to take place.

Conclusion

Treatment for obesity in children and adolescents is complex and challenging. It often requires the cooperation of the entire family. It ultimately should employ cognitive and behavioral strategies that help children and adolescents make the lifestyle changes necessary to become healthier as they develop. Moreover, interventions should consider any psychological diagnoses the children and adolescents may have as well as making sure underserved populations are addressed sensitively. In addition, the childhood obesity epidemic is a community, national, and global problem. Communities and governments should continue to improve to make it easier for families to live healthier, longer lives.

CHAPTER 5

Case Studies

Case Study #1

Gabriela is a five-year-old Hispanic girl who is 3'6" and weighs 55 pounds, which puts her in the above 95th percentile and is considered obese. She presents to the psychologist for weight-loss assistance. The following information comes from Gabriela, her mother, and her medical records.

Medical: Gabriela's doctor notes that she is concerned about her weight, particularly since it has led her to be more easily out of breath and has made it more difficult to engage in physical activity. She is also concerned that Gabriela is not obtaining the nutrients she needs on a daily basis. However, she does not have any noted serious medical problems, pain, or changes in sleep.

Weight or body or health behaviors: Gabriela's weight has been in the normal range up until a year ago when her family moved from Mexico to the United States. Others in her family and her community have also experienced weight gain; as such, Gabriela does not seem to have an awareness of her changing body. Gabriela's diet currently consists of mostly fast food and processed food. She typically eats sugar-sweetened cereals and juice for breakfast; hot lunches at school, and fast food for dinner. It appears she is only getting about one serving of fruits and vegetables per day. Regarding physical activity, Gabriela sits down a lot at recess and watches television or reads when she comes home.

Psychological: Gabriela does not seem to have any significant symptoms of depression, anxiety, or anger. However, she has begun to demonstrate behavioral problems at school due to her lack of participation at recess and due to her lack of concentration at school.

Psychosocial: Gabriela's parents are married, and she has two older brothers and one younger sister. Her parents immigrated to Texas from Mexico a year ago, and they have all experienced weight gain since moving. Gabriela's family are of low socioeconomic status, and they live in a neighborhood that does not have easy access to healthy grocery stores or safe parks. Gabriela's parents both work full-time, and her brothers watch her when she comes home from school. She has two friends in school. Her family also regularly attends church, so she has a strong community support.

Her school performance began strong when she started kindergarten, but she has become increasingly distracted throughout the school year. Gabriela is not involved in any structured extracurricular activities; however, her family spends time together on the weekend to go to movies and to church.

Positive: Gabriela is intelligent, kind, and curious. She wants to perform better in school and wants to grow up to be an astronaut. Gabriela's family is strong, hardworking, and resilient.

Discussion Questions

What additional questionnaires would you recommend for the assessment? What treatment would you recommend?

Case Study #1 Recommendations

Additional Questionnaires

Children's Version of the Eating Attitudes Test

Treatment Recommendations

- Operant conditioning
  - Teach parents how to use positive reinforcement to increase Gabriela's health behaviors; for example, Gabriela gets a sticker when she eats one serving of vegetables.
  - Teach parents how to use negative punishment to reduce Gabriela's unhealthy behaviors; for example, if Gabriela watches television for more than one hour per day, then she will not be able to watch television for a week.

- Modeling
  - Teach parents to model healthy behaviors for their children by working out, going for walks, and eating fruits and vegetables.
  - Encourage parents to teach their older children to be models for healthy snacks and active behaviors after school.
  - Expose her to examples of active public figures; for example, Laurie Hernandez is a famous Latina gymnast.
- Stimulus control
  - Advise parents to purge any unhealthy foods in the house and to make fruit and vegetables easily accessible in the home such as having a fruit bowl or cut up carrots in fun shapes in the refrigerator.
  - Have limits on television watching to one hour per day.
- Dietary interventions
  - Have family track their food behaviors for one week and make suggested modifications; for example, instead of eating fast food in the evenings, have the family prepare meals on Sunday for the week and give each child a job in helping with food preparation.
  - Teach the family the "Traffic Light system" and the "Choose My Plate" guidelines to help Gabriela learn about which foods she should limit and which foods she should consume regularly.
  - Eat meals together as much as possible as a family and demonstrate mindful eating; for example, her parents can make statements while eating such as "I'm beginning to feel full, so I should stop eating."
  - Encourage parents to avoid the words "diet" and "good or bad" food.
- Physical activity interventions
  - Show Gabriela how to use "Instant Recess" on YouTube and have her participate at least once per day for vigorous activity.
  - Go for family walks weeknights or on the weekend.

- ○ Have family jump-rope contests.
- ○ Sign Gabriela up for a physical extracurricular activity such as dance or basketball and see if other parents are to carpool if work prohibits picking up or dropping off daily.
- ○ Take family to a safe park on the weekends, so children can engage in more muscle-strengthening activities like climbing up the playground or going on the monkey bars.
- • Community-specific interventions
  - ○ Refer the family to *promotoras* or *curanderos* for additional assistance.
  - ○ Give family a list of healthy options in their community and ways to become involved in community activities such as a "town 5k."
- • Other
  - ○ Monitor Gabriela's nutrition intake and see if it affects her concentration at school and school performance; if it does not, then Gabriela will likely need a psychological evaluation to assess other possibilities such as Attention Deficit Hyperactivity Disorder (ADHD).

Case Study #2

James is an eight-year-old Caucasian male who is 4'2" and weighs 110 pounds, which puts him above the 95th percentile and is considered obese. His parents are bringing him in for weight-loss assistance as per his physician's recommendations; however, it is clear that James and his parents do not want to make any major changes in their lifestyle.

Medical: James has high blood pressure, and his physician is concerned about his increasing weight. It is also difficult for him to engage in physical activity at times.

Weight or body or health behaviors: James' weight has always been higher than normal for his age, but his rate of weight gain has steadily increased each year. He does not appear to notice or care about his changing weight. His parents stated that they let him eat whatever he wants, so his typical meal is sugary cereal or cookies for breakfast; two lunchables for lunch with two desserts; chips, cookies, ice cream, or cake for snacks; and pizza, fast food, or frozen meals for dinner. He also almost exclusively drinks regular soda for all meals. He does not engage in any regular exercise other than walking around school. In fact, most of his spare time is spent playing video games and watching television.

Psychological: James does not present with any major anxiety or depressive symptoms. However, his parents indicated that he has gotten in trouble at school for being a "bully" toward other children and acting aggressively. His teacher told them that he would take other children's food or threaten to hurt them. His parents indicated that he is the largest child in his class, so they think the teacher is being unnecessarily hard on him. James presents more egocentric than is typical for his age, and his attitude indicated that he expected to get what he wanted most of the time. His parents stated that the only way they can get him to do something he doesn't want to do is through bribery, which typically involves food.

Psychosocial: James lives with his parents and does not have any other siblings. James' parents indicate that they believe in "free" and "nurturing" parenting and let James make his own choices. It is clear that James' parents are warm and caring toward James, yet they do not have any rules or structure for him, suggesting a clear permissive parenting style. James is not able to name any friends at school or in his neighborhood, and it appears he spends his time alone watching television or engaging in other sedentary behaviors.

Positive: James is intelligent and somewhat independent, and he feels loved by his parents. James also likes superheroes.

Discussion Questions

What additional questionnaires would you recommend for the assessment? What treatment would you recommend?

Case Study #2 Recommendations

Additional Questionnaires

Children's Version of the Eating Attitudes Test

Treatment

- Motivational interviewing for parents
  - ○ James' parents do not want to make any major changes in their life. However, they care about their son and do want him to be healthier. Therefore, motivational interviewing can help increase their desire to make the lifestyle changes necessary to help their son.
  - ○ James may benefit from simple motivational interviewing by figuring out his values and making the link between behaviors that will lead to his values; for example, if he does not want to go to the doctor or get in trouble at school, then the behaviors to reduce those unwanted outcomes can be of focus.
- Operant conditioning
  - ○ Home: James is clearly in charge at home and is not disciplined. Therefore, it is important to establish clear rules and consequences at home. Healthy choices and behaviors will be rewarded with nonfood related reinforcers such as small toys or tokens to earn a trip to the pool. His parents will have the challenge of negatively punishing undesired behaviors by taking away something of value; for example, if James sneaks candy, then he is not allowed to watch television or play video games for the next several days. His parents will need to be educated about how to handle any tantrums and how to follow through with consequences.
  - ○ School: Rules at home should carry over to school. The parents should meet with the teacher to obtain more details on James' behavior at school. They should communicate with the teacher and James that the rules apply at school and have the teacher follow-through with rewards for positive behaviors and negative consequences for negative behaviors.
- Stimulus control
  - ○ James appears to have very low self-control. Therefore, his parents can help him be more successful in engaging in healthy behaviors by removing temptations. All junk food

should be eliminated from the home and replaced with healthy options. James can still be allowed to choose what he wants to eat, but he can only choose from healthy options.

- Dietary interventions
  - James' parents should be educated about nutritional requirements and portion sizes that are appropriate for their son. The stoplight system, however, may not the best option for James because he may focus more on the restricted foods since he is used to getting what he wants. Therefore, the parents could buy only healthy foods and tell him that those foods will make him stronger like a superhero. In addition, he could be given several options for each meal but not be directly told they are "healthier" than the previous food.
  - Another strategy to increase his healthy food consumption would be to make eating healthy food fun and like a game. For example, make fun shapes out of healthy food and make preferred foods like spaghetti with vegetables (e.g., spaghetti squash).
- Physical activity interventions
  - His sedentary video games could be switched out for a Nintendo Wii or Pokemon Go, which would allow him to have fun with video games while obtaining exercise.
  - Since James likes superheroes, the parents could start by setting up daily "superhero training" where James could engage in exercises that would make him fast and strong like a superhero.
  - Since James does not have any friends, having James pick out a sport to start would allow him to exercise as well as develop relationships.
- Other
  - Empathy and communication skills training: James' bullying behavior suggests a lack of empathy for others and inability to communicate effectively with his peers. Therefore, he would benefit from empathy training to understand the importance of being sensitive to others and

how to do so. He would also likely benefit from learn more effective ways to communicate his needs with others than through aggression.

Case Study #3

Latisha is a 13-year-old African American girl who is 4'11" and weighs 145 pounds, which puts her in the above 95th percentile and is considered obese. She presents to the psychologist for weight loss assistance. Latisha and her parents are willing to make any changes to help with weight loss.

Medical: Latisha has high blood pressure and has Type 2 diabetes. Her weight continues to rise despite attempts at weight loss. Her weight has also led to knee and back pain and insomnia.

Weight or body or health behaviors: Latisha indicated that she has always struggled with her weight, but she has gained more weight rapidly since she began puberty around 10 to 11 years of age. She stated that she dislikes her body and has a hard time finding clothes that fit her well. She indicated that she has learned a lot about healthy eating at school and from her mother, but she noted that she continues to gain weight. She described eating whole grain cereal for breakfast; a healthy sandwich, fruit, and crackers for lunch; 100-calorie packaged snacks; and whatever her parents make for dinner, which is usually hearty but healthy. She noted that she eats the same size meals as her family, and her brothers are lean, so she does not understand why is she gaining weight. She indicated that she also goes for at least a 30-minute walk a day, but she does not engage in any vigorous exercise. She noted that her friends invite her to go to Zumba classes, and she wants to go but she doesn't due to being self-conscious about her body.

Psychological: Latisha described experiencing significant depression. She endorsed symptoms of depressed mood, anhedonia, reduced energy, irritability, difficulty sleeping, feelings of worthlessness, and feelings of hopelessness. She endorsed having a particularly low sense of self- and body-esteem. She denied any suicidal ideation, intent, or plan, however.

Psychosocial: Latisha's parents are married, and she has two older brothers. She noted that her father and brothers are a normal weight, but she and her mother are obese. She described having a positive, supportive family. Latisha loves math and is making straight As at school. She also has several good friends who are supportive of her.

Positive: Latisha is excelling at school and has significant support.

Discussion Questions

What additional questionnaires would you recommend for the assessment? What treatment would you recommend?

Case Study #3 Recommendations

Additional Questionnaires

Body Esteem Scale
Body Shape Questionnaire
Children's Depression Inventory
Piers-Harris Self-Concept Scale 2

Treatment

- Dietary interventions
  - While Latisha appears to be eating healthy foods, it looks like she may not be eating enough protein, which may be causing her to eat more foods. Moreover, she may be eating healthy foods but too large of portion sizes. For example, she noted that she is eating the same amount as her older, lean brothers, but they need a lot more calories than she needs; therefore, she is likely overeating.
  - Latisha may benefit from learning about "Choose My Plate" to make sure she is getting enough variety and attending to her portion sizes.

- Physical activity interventions
  - Latisha appears to be getting mild to moderate exercise; however, she is not getting vigorous exercise, which should make an impact on her weight loss. She is interested in Zumba but feels self-conscious. Therefore, it is recommended that she start first following free Zumba on YouTube until she gets comfortable with the pace and the steps. Next, she can go to a smaller, Zumba class likely at a least popular time, so she can get comfortable exercising in front of only a few others. She can then work toward attending a large Zumba class with her friends.
  - Latisha may also benefit from joining a sports team where she would get regular, vigorous activity under the supervision of a coach.
- Treatment for Major Depressive Disorder (MDD)
  - Latisha has MDD; therefore, she would benefit from cognitive-behavioral therapy to reduce her symptoms. In particular, she would benefit from assistance in increasing her self- and body-esteem. For example, she could complete exercises that emphasize what she does like about her body as well as focus on the function of her body (e.g., her strong legs allow her to walk fast).
  - Latisha may benefit from a support group for other young women who have lower body esteem and depression.
  - Latisha's depressive symptoms should be monitored to make sure they don't escalate.
- Community-based interventions
  - Latisha is on the upper end of the "Girls on the Run" group (ages 8 to 13 years) that is designed to empower girls through exercise. However, she could get started in the group and then perhaps become a leader in the group once she has aged out.

Case Study #4

Mason is a 17-year-old multiethnic male adolescent who is 5'9" and weighs 220 pounds, which puts him above the 95th percentile and is considered obese. He is being evaluated by the psychologist for prebariatric surgery. The following information comes from Mason, his mother, and his medical records.

Surgery: Mason is being considered for a Roux-en Y gastric bypass by Dr. Johnson. He was recommended for bariatric surgery due to his comorbid conditions; he has Type 2 diabetes, obstructive sleep apnea, high blood pressure, high cholesterol, and cardiovascular problems. He has been considering bariatric surgery for the past year.

Weight: Mason indicated that he has struggled with his weight since kindergarten. He indicated that he steadily gained weight and then had a higher rate of weight gain over the past two years. He attributed his weight gain to genetics, poor eating habits, and lack of physical activity. He expressed that his weight has interfered with his physical, emotional, social, and academic functioning. Specifically, he noted that he has difficulty getting around his school due to becoming out of breath, described feeling depressed and angry as a result of his weight, noted having few friends because of his weight, and expressed that he has difficulty focusing on his schoolwork since he thinks about his weight most of the time. He stated that he has tried an assortment of diets from Weight Watchers to Nutrisystem to low carb diets, but he noted that none have been effective long term. He stated that on Weight Watchers, he lost 15 pounds over one month, but he noted that he gained it back when he could not maintain the diet restrictions. While he denied using any maladaptive strategies to lose weight such as vomiting and taking laxatives, he indicated that he has frequent episodes of binge eating. He stated that he can eat up to 1,000 calories within an hour and feels like he can control this behavior. He indicated that he engages this behavior almost every weekday when he gets home from school. He noted that he does not binge eat as frequently on the weekend as his mother is around most of the time. He described struggling with binge eating for the past two years.

Health behaviors: Mason stated that he typically eats French toast sticks for breakfast, pizza and fries at the school cafeteria for lunch, and meat, vegetable, or starch for dinner (based on what his mother makes). He indicated that he snacks frequently on chips and cookies, which he has easy access to at home. He indicated that he typically drinks orange juice with breakfast and then drinks regular Coke the rest of the day. He denied engaging in any regular physical activity other than walking to his classes at school. He noted that he cannot easily engage in exercise due to his weight and medical problems. However, he indicated that if he was physically able, then he would want to play basketball.

Preparedness: Mason indicated that his aunt had bariatric surgery five years ago, so she has been his main source of information. He described understanding that he would have to eat more protein and cut back on carbohydrates. He also stated that he knows he will have to cut out the Cokes and fried food. He expressed understanding that the surgery could result in death or infection. He stated that he has the support of his mother and extended family and that his mother would be making changes with him. He expressed the biggest obstacle being giving up Cokes. He denied implementing any changes yet. He expressed that he hopes to lose 80 pounds as a result of the surgery.

Psychological functioning: Mason noted that he becomes depressed at times due to his weight, but he denied having any suicidal ideation, intent, or plan. He described having low self-esteem, however, and problems with his body image. Mason denied having any previous psychological disorders. He also denied taking psychotropic medications previously or attending counseling.

Medical or substance use history: As previously stated, Mason has Type 2 diabetes, obstructive sleep apnea, high blood pressure, high cholesterol, and cardiovascular problems. He denied any use of nicotine, alcohol, or recreational drugs.

Psychosocial history: Mason indicated that he currently lives with his mother. He stated that his father left him when he was one-year-old and is not in his life. He denied having any siblings. However, he noted that he has two aunts and two uncles on the maternal side and spends time with them and their families at times on the weekend. He stated that he is home alone typically when he gets home from school until his mother gets home from work. Mason indicated that he is an average performing student. He denied engaging in any structured extracurricular activities.

Positive: Mason is a kind, caring person. He enjoys drawing and writing.

Discussion Questions

What additional questionnaires would you recommend?
Would you recommend him for bariatric surgery?
Any other treatment recommendations?

Case Study #4 Recommendations

Additional Questionnaires

Questionnaire of Eating and Weight Patterns—Adolescent Version
Body Esteem Scale
Body Shape Questionnaire
Children's Depression Inventory
Piers-Harris Self-Concept Scale 2

Candidacy for Bariatric Surgery

Based on his multiple comorbid conditions and lack of effectiveness of other weight loss strategies, Mason is an overall good candidate for bariatric surgery. However, he has Binge Eating Disorder (BED), which could make it dangerous for him to undergo bariatric surgery until it is under control. Therefore, I recommend that he does not undergo bariatric surgery until he has seen a psychologist for counseling for his BED and until he no longer meets criteria for it.

Further Recommendations Include

- Cognitive-behavioral therapy for BED
  - Teach Mason how to become more aware of his hunger and satiety signals using mindfulness.
  - Teach Mason healthy coping strategies to use in lieu of binge eating, particularly strategies that are incompatible with eating (e.g., playing a game on his phone, walking around the house while listening to music).

- o Use cognitive restructuring to work through cognitive distortions about eating and his body image.
- o Enroll Mason in a structured after-school extracurricular activity about his interests related to drawing and writing that has transportation to extinguish the habit of after-school binging; this recommendation would also likely increase the number of friends Mason has for support.
- Monitor depressive symptoms
  - o Mason does not have MDD, but he does experience some depressive symptoms, so any exacerbations should be noted.
- Stimulus control
  - o Advise Mason to get rid of all unhealthy foods in the house and begin eating at one location in the house—at the kitchen table with no distractions.
  - o Have Mason put free weights by the couch and put remote control or technological devices in hard-to-reach places.
- Dietary interventions
  - o Have Mason plan for yogurt, fruit, and granola for breakfast; pack a healthy lunch the night before; continue eating healthy meals for dinner with his mother; and have vegetables and low calorie options (e.g., popsicle) as snacks.
  - o Teach Mason how to cook his own healthy food, how to portion out serving sizes, and other nutritional education.
- Physical activity interventions
  - o Since physical activity can be taxing for Mason, a great low-impact exercise is swimming. Refer him to a local program to get started slow and gradually increase in length and intensity.
  - o Have Mason incorporate small increases in daily activity such as walking around during commercials, standing on one foot when brushing his teeth, and using a standing desk for homework.
- Family therapy
  - o Since Mason's father left when he was young, he may have some concerns he needs to express in therapy. Moreover,

his mother will likely benefit from being part of the process and create an environment where he can be more successful with healthy behaviors.

Case Study #5

The Wells family presents for family-based weight loss assistance. The Wells family is a blended family consisting of Paige (mother) and her 15-year-old daughter and 7-year-old son and Wallace (father) consisting of a 12-year-old son, and a 5-year-old son. Paige and Wallace both met three years ago and moved in together a year ago. Everyone in the family is obese and appears motivated to engage in weight loss.

Medical: Paige and Wallace both have high blood pressure, Type 2 diabetes, and obstructive sleep apnea. While their children do not have any major medical conditions, their family physician is concerned about the entire family's health due to obesity.

Weight or body or health behaviors: Everyone in the family has typically been overweight, but they have all gained weight at an increasing rate since moving into the same household a year ago. Body image concerns are not a problem within the family since everyone's size appears "normal" within the family. However, they are all concerned about their weight for health purposes. Typical eating consists of donuts or McDonald's for breakfast; fast food for parents or hot lunches at school for the children; and frozen meals or fast food for dinner. Snacks consist of chips, brownies, and granola bars. The family drinks juice or regular soda for most meals. The family loves to watch movies and television shows together, but no one engages in any regular physical activity.

Psychological: No one in family exhibits any major symptoms of psychological disorders. However, Paige is becoming increasingly anxious about her family's health.

Psychosocial: The family has been living together for the past year in a new city, and it has been a difficult transition, in particular for Paige's 15-year-old daughter. Her daughter doesn't like having only brothers and having to share a bathroom with boys. The three sons fight constantly and are often competing for attention from the parents. All the children were initially upset about having to leave their friends and school to start over in a new location. In addition, Paige and Wallace have experienced some conflict on what rules to enforce for the children; Paige is more strict, and Wallace is more lenient. They also have no extended family in the area and are mostly on their own in a new city.

Positive: The family loves one another and all appear motivated to make changes.

Discussion Question

What treatment would you recommend for the family?

Case Study #5 Recommendations

All treatments in this section will be framed toward family-based treatment.

- Family therapy
  - Since this is a recent blended family, Paige and Wallace would likely benefit from working with a psychologist on establishing consistent rules and consequences for the family. Moreover, having the family share concerns and ways to compromise during sessions can likely help decrease conflict and attention concerns.
  - Family therapy would result in shared goals, so everyone can help each other and feel they are on the same team. To that end, making sure the family has weekly family outings or meetings that help everyone connect is important.
- Group family therapy
  - The Wells family would likely benefit from attending a group-based family treatment. This type of treatment usually consists of a weekly session with other families who are trying to lose weight. Often, the group is split into "parent sessions" and "child sessions." That is, parents would learn from a facilitator about making lifestyle changes at home and the children would be led into making healthy choices as well as engaging in physical activity during the group time. The families would then come together at the end,

share knowledge, and establish family health goals for the coming week.

- ○ Group family therapy would have an added benefit of allowing the Wells family to easily make friends in the area who would also be making changes with them.
- Community-based interventions
  - ○ Since the family does not know many people in the area, they would likely benefit from getting involved with active community programs such as a town 5k or building a community garden.
  - ○ The family may want to get involved with the school about how to provide healthy meals and physical activity for their children.

References

Abbott, R.A., A.J. Lee, C.O. Stubbs, and P.S.W. Davies. 2010. "Accuracy of Weight Status Perception in Contemporary Australian Children and Adolescents." *Journal of Paediatrics and Child Health* 46, no. 6, pp. 343–48. doi:10.1111/j.1440-1754.2010.01719.x

Alfonzo, M.A. 2005. "To Walk or Not to Walk? The Hierarchy of Walking Needs." *Environment and Behavior* 37, no. 6, pp. 808–36. doi:10.1177/0013916504274016

American Psychiatric Association. 2013. *Diagnostic and Statistical Manual of Mental Disorders*. 5th ed. Washington, DC: American Psychiatric Association.

Bates, B., and M.R. Stone. 2015. "Measures of Outdoor Play and Independent Mobility in Children and Youth: A Methodological Review." *Journal of Science and Medicine in Sport* 18, no. 5, pp. 545–52. doi:10.1016/j.jsams.2014.07.006

Baym, C.L., N.A. Khan, J.M. Monti, L.B. Raine, E.S. Drollette, R.D. Moore, M.R. Scudder, A.F. Kramer, C.H. Hillman, and N.J. Cohen. 2014. "Dietary Lipids Are Differentially Associated with Hippocampal-Dependent Relational Memory in Prepubescent Children." *The American Journal of Clinical Nutrition* 99, no. 5, pp. 1026–32. doi:10.3945/ajcn.113.079624

Beech, B.M., and M.M. Jernigan. 2014. "Is That All There Is? A Comprehensive Review of Obesity Prevention and Treatment Interventions for African American Girls." In *Obesity Interventions in Underserved Communities: Evidence and Directions*, eds. V.M. Brennan, S.K. Kumanyika, and R.E. Zambrana, 63–76. Baltimore, MD: Johns Hopkins University Press.

Bishop-Gilyard, C.T., R.I. Berkowitz, T.A. Wadden, C.A. Gehrman, J.L. Cronquist, and R.H. Moore. 2011. "Weight Reduction in Obese Adolescents with and without Binge Eating." *Obesity* 19, no. 5, pp. 982–87. doi:10.1038/oby.2010.249

Bolen, S., E. Tseng, S. Hutfless, J.B. Segal, C. Suarez-Cuervo, Z. Berger, L.M. Wilson, Y. Chu, E. Iyoha, and N.M. Maruthur. 2016. *Diabetes Medications for Adults With Type 2 Diabetes: An Update*. AHRQ Comparative Effectiveness Reviews. Rockville (MD): Agency for Healthcare Research and Quality (US). www.ncbi.nlm.nih.gov/books/NBK362863/

Branch, R.A., A.L. Chester, S. Hanks, S. Kuhn, M. McMillion, C. Morton-McSwain, S. Paulsen, U. Kiran Para, Y. Cannon, and S.J. Groark. 2014. "Obesity Management Organized by Adolescents in Rural Appalachia."

In *Obesity Interventions in Underserved Communities: Evidence and Directions*, eds. V.M. Brennan, S.K. Kumanyika, and R.E. Zambrana, 205–12. Baltimore, MD: Johns Hopkins University Press.

Butcher, J.N., C.L. Williams, J.R. Graham, R.P. Archer, A. Tellegen, Y.S. Ben-Porath, and B. Kaemmer. 1992. *MMPI-A (Minnesota Multiphasic Personality Inventory—Adolescent): Manual for Administration, Scoring, and Interpretation.* Minneapolis: University of Minnesota Press.

Cani, P.D., and N.M. Delzenne. 2009. "The Role of the Gut Microbiota in Energy Metabolism and Metabolic Disease." *Current Pharmaceutical Design* 15, no. 13, pp. 1546–58.

Center for Disease Control. 2016a. "Body Mass Index." www.cdc.gov/healthyweight/assessing/bmi/

Center for Disease Control. 2016b. "Childhood Overweight and Obesity." www.cdc.gov/obesity/data/childhood.html

Center for Disease Control. 2016c. "How Much Physical Activity Do Children Need?" www.cdc.gov/physicalactivity/basics/children/index.htm

Center for Disease Control. 2016d. "MAPPS Interventions for Communities Putting Prevention to Work." www.cdc.gov/chronicdisease/recovery/pdf/mapps_intervention_table.pdf

Center for Disease Control. 2016e. "Physical Activity Facts." www.cdc.gov/healthyschools/physicalactivity/facts.htm

Challis, B.G., and G.W.M. Millington. 1993. "Proopiomelanocortin Deficiency." In *GeneReviews®*, eds. R.A. Pagon, M.P. Adam, H.H. Ardinger, S.E. Wallace, A. Amemiya, L.J.H. Bean, T.D. Bird, C.T. Fong, H.C. Mefford, R.J.H. Smith, and K. Stephens. Seattle, WA: University of Washington. www.ncbi.nlm.nih.gov/books/NBK174451/

Chambers, E.C., M. Pichardo, and N. Davis. 2014. "Dietary Acculturation in U.S. Hispanic Communities." In *Obesity Interventions in Underserved Communities: Evidence and Directions*, eds. V.M. Brennan, S.K. Kumanyika, and R.E. Zambrana, 80–102. Baltimore, MD: Johns Hopkins University Press.

Chanoine, J.P., and M. Richard. 2011. "Early Weight Loss and Outcome at One Year in Obese Adolescents Treated with Orlistat or Placebo." *International Journal of Pediatric Obesity* 6, no. 2, pp. 95–101. doi:10.3109/17477166.2010.519387

Christofaro, D., S.M. Andrade, R.A. Fernandes, M.A.S. Cabrera, F. Rodríguez-Artalejo, and A.E. Mesas. January 2016. "Overweight Parents Are Twice as Likely to Underestimate the Weight of Their Teenage Children, Regardless of Their Socio-Demographic Characteristics." *Acta Paediatrica* 105, no. 10, pp. e474–e479. doi:10.1111/apa.13342

Cohen, D.A. 2014. *A Big Fat Crisis: The Hidden Forces Behind the Obesity Epidemic and How We Can End It.* New York: Nation Books.

Cohen, M.J., and G.A. Datto. 2015. "Ethical Considerations in Adolescent Bariatric Surgery: A Case Presentation." *Clinical Practice in Pediatric Psychology,* Ethics and Pediatrics 3, no. 4, pp. 365–69. doi:10.1037/cpp0000121

Cole, T.J. 2007. "Early Causes of Child Obesity and Implications for Prevention." *Acta Paediatrica* 96, no. 454, pp. 2–4. doi:10.1111/j.1651-2227.2007.00162.x

Cooper, P.J., M.J. Taylor, Z. Cooper, and C.G. Fairbum. 1987. "The Development and Validation of the Body Shape Questionnaire." *International Journal of Eating Disorders* 6, no. 4, pp. 485–94. doi:10.1002/1098-108X(198707)6:4<485::AID-EAT2260060405>3.0.CO;2-O

Cox, L. 2009. "Courts Charge Mother of 555-Pound Boy." *abc News,* June 29. http://abcnews.go.com/Health/WellnessNews/story?id=7941609

Datz, T. 2013. "Poll Finds Lack of Physical Education in Public Schools a Concern of Parents | News | Harvard T.H. Chan School of Public Health." www.hsph.harvard.edu/news/press-releases/lack-of-physical-education-in-schools-concerns-parents/

Davison, K.K., and L.L. Birch. 2002. "Processes Linking Weight Status and Self-Concept among Girls from Ages 5 to 7 Years." *Developmental Psychology* 38, no. 5, pp. 735–48. doi:10.1037/0012-1649.38.5.735

Decaluwé, V., C. Braet, and C.G. Fairburn. 2003. "Binge Eating in Obese Children and Adolescents." *International Journal of Eating Disorders* 33, no. 1, pp. 78–84. doi:10.1002/eat.10110

de Vargas Zanini, R., I.S. Santos, M.A.D. Chrestani, and D.P. Gigante. 2015. "Body Fat in Children Measured by DXA, Air-Displacement Plethysmography, TBW and Multicomponent Models: A Systematic Review." *Maternal and Child Health Journal* 19, no. 7, pp. 1567–73. doi:10.1007/s10995-015-1666-5

Dykens, E. 2000. "Contaminated and Unusual Food Combinations: What Do People with Prader-Willi Syndrome Choose?" *Mental Retardation* 38, no. 2, pp. 163–71. doi:10.1352/0047-6765(2000)038<0163:CAUFCW>2.0. CO;2

Dykens, E., and B. Shah. 2003. "Psychiatric Disorders in Prader-Willi Syndrome: Epidemiology and Management." *CNS Drugs* 17, no. 3, pp. 167–78.

Eisenberg, M.E., D. Neumark-Sztainer, and M. Story. 2003. "Associations of Weight-Based Teasing and Emotional Well-Being among Adolescents." *Archives of Pediatrics & Adolescent Medicine* 157, no. 8, pp. 733–38. doi:10.1001/archpedi.157.8.733

Epstein, L.H., R.A. Paluch, M.D. Beecher, and J.N. Roemmich. 2008. "Increasing Healthy Eating vs. Reducing High Energy-Dense Foods to Treat Pediatric Obesity." *Obesity (Silver Spring, Md.)* 16, no. 2, pp. 318–26. doi:10.1038/oby.2007.61

Evans, C., and B. Dolan. 1993. "Body Shape Questionnaire: Derivation of Shortened 'Alternative Forms.'" *International Journal of Eating Disorders* 13, no. 3, pp. 315–21. doi:10.1002/1098-108X(199304)13:3<315::AID-EAT2260130310>3.0.CO;2-3

Fani, L., S. Bak, P. Delhanty, E.F.C. van Rossum, and E.L.T. van den Akker. 2014. "The Melanocortin-4 Receptor as Target for Obesity Treatment: A Systematic Review of Emerging Pharmacological Therapeutic Options." *International Journal of Obesity* 38, no. 2, pp. 163–69. doi:10.1038/ijo.2013.80

Farley, T.A., E.T. Baker, L. Futrell, and J.C. Rice. 2010. "The Ubiquity of Energy-Dense Snack Foods: A National Multicity Study." *American Journal of Public Health* 100, no. 2, pp. 306–11. doi:10.2105/AJPH.2009.178681

Fawcett, K.A., and I. Barroso. 2010. "The Genetics of Obesity: FTO Leads the Way." *Trends in Genetics* 26, no. 6, pp. 266–74. doi:10.1016/j.tig.2010.02.006

Fletcher, J.M., D.E. Frisvold, and N. Tefft. 2011. "Are Soft Drink Taxes an Effective Mechanism for Reducing Obesity?" *Journal of Policy Analysis and Management* 30 no. 3, pp. 655–62. doi:10.1002/pam.20582

Fothergill, E., J. Guo, L. Howard, J.C. Kerns, N.D. Knuth, R. Brychta, K.Y. Chen, M.C. Skarulis, M. Walter, P.J. Walter, and K.D. Hall. May 2016. "Persistent Metabolic Adaptation 6 Years after 'The Biggest Loser' Competition." *Obesity (Silver Spring, Md.)* 24, no. 8, pp. 1612–19. doi:10.1002/oby.21538

Goodman, E., B.R. Hinden, and S. Khandelwal. 2000. "Accuracy of Teen and Parental Reports of Obesity and Body Mass Index." *Pediatrics* 106, no. 1, pp. 52–58.

Gortmaker, S.L., A. Must, J.M. Perrin, A.M. Sobol, and W.H. Dietz. 1993. "Social and Economic Consequences of Overweight in Adolescence and Young Adulthood." *The New England Journal of Medicine* 329, no. 14, pp. 1008–12. doi:10.1056/NEJM199309303291406

Greening, L., K.T. Harrell, A.K. Low, and C.E. Fielder. 2011. "Efficacy of a School-Based Childhood Obesity Intervention Program in a Rural Southern Community: TEAM Mississippi Project." *Obesity* 19, no. 6, pp. 1213–19. doi:10.1038/oby.2010.329

Greenwald, A.G., D.E. McGhee, and J.L. Schwartz. 1998. "Measuring Individual Differences in Implicit Cognition: The Implicit Association Test." *Journal of Personality and Social Psychology* 74, no. 6, pp. 1464–80.

Higginson, A.D., J.M. McNamara, and A.I. Houston. 2016. "Fatness and Fitness: Exposing the Logic of Evolutionary Explanations for Obesity." *Proceedings of the Royal Society B: Biological Sciences* 283, no. 1822, p. 20152443. doi:10.1098/rspb.2015.2443

Hilbert, A., T. Hildebrandt, W.S. Agras, D.E. Wilfley, and G.T. Wilson. 2015. "Rapid Response in Psychological Treatments for Binge Eating Disorder." *Journal of Consulting and Clinical Psychology* 83, no. 3, pp. 649–54. doi:10.1037/ccp0000018

Hillstrom, K.A., and J.K. Graves. 2015. "A Review of Depression and Quality of Life Outcomes in Adolescents Post Bariatric Surgery." *Journal of Child and Adolescent Psychiatric Nursing* 28, no. 1, pp. 50–59. doi:10.1111/jcap.12104

Hollar, D., M. Lombardo, G. Lopez-Mitnik, T.L. Hollar, M. Almon, A.S. Agatston, and S.E. Messiah. 2010. "Effective Multi-Level, Multi-Sector, School-Based Obesity Prevention Programming Improves Weight, Blood Pressure, and Academic Performance, Especially among Low-Income, Minority Children." *Journal of Health Care for the Poor and Underserved* 21, no. 2, pp. 93–108. doi:10.1353/hpu.0.0304

Inge, T.H., M.H. Zeller, T.M. Jenkins, M. Helmrath, M.L. Brandt, M.P. Michalsky, C.M. Harmon, A. Courcoulas, M. Horlick, S.A. Xanthakos, L. Dolan, M. Mitsnefes, S.J. Barnett, R. Buncher, and Teen-LABS Consotrium. 2014. "Perioperative Outcomes of Adolescents Undergoing Bariatric Surgery: The Teen-Longitudinal Assessment of Bariatric Surgery (Teen-LABS) Study." *JAMA Pediatrics* 168, no. 1, pp. 47–53. doi:10.1001/jamapediatrics.2013.4296

Johnson, W.G., F.G. Grieve, C.D. Adams, and J. Sandy. 1999. "Measuring Binge Eating in Adolescents: Adolescent and Parent Versions of the Questionnaire of Eating and Weight Patterns." *International Journal of Eating Disorders* 26, no. 3, pp. 301–14. doi:10.1002/(SICI)1098-108X(199911)26:3<301::AID-EAT8>3.0.CO;2-M

Johnston, C.A., C. Tyler, G. Fullerton, B.K. McFarlin, W.S.C. Poston, C.K. Haddock, R.S. Reeves, and J.P. Foreyt. 2010. "Effects of a School-Based Weight Maintenance Program for Mexican-American Children: Results at 2 Years." *Obesity (Silver Spring, Md.)* 18, no. 3, pp. 542–47. doi:10.1038/oby.2009.241

Kalarchian, M.A., and M.D. Marcus. 2012. "Psychiatric Comorbidity of Childhood Obesity." *International Review of Psychiatry* 24, no. 3, pp. 241–46. doi:10.3109/09540261.2012.678818

Kaplan, M.S., N. Huguet, J.T. Newsom, and B.H. McFarland. 2004. "The Association between Length of Residence and Obesity among Hispanic Immigrants." *American Journal of Preventive Medicine* 27, no. 4, pp. 323–26. doi:10.1016/j.amepre.2004.07.005

Kazaks, A.G., and J.S. Stern. 2013. *Nutrition and Obesity: Assessment, Management, and Prevention.* Burlington, MA: Jones & Bartlett Learning.

Kirkland, A. 2008. "Think of the Hippopotamus: Rights Consciousness in the Fat Acceptance Movement." *Law & Society Review* 42, no. 2, pp. 397–431. doi:10.1111/j.1540-5893.2008.00346.x

Kopp, C.B. 1982. "Antecedents of Self-Regulation: A Developmental Perspective." *Developmental Psychology* 18, no. 2, pp. 199–214. doi:10.1037/0012-1649.18.2.199

Kovacs, M. 1992. *Children's Depression Inventory*. Toronto, ON: Multi-Health Systems.

Kristeller, J.L., and R.Q. Wolever. 2014. "Mindfulness-Based Eating Awareness Training: Treatment of Overeating and Obesity." In *Mindfulness-Based Treatment Approaches: Clinician's Guide to Evidence Base and Applications*, ed. R.A. Baer, 119–39. 2nd ed. San Diego, CA: Elsevier Academic Press.

Le Chatelier, E., T. Nielsen, J. Qin, E. Prifti, F. Hildebrand, G. Falony, M. Almeida, M. Arumugam, J.M. Batto, S. Kennedy, P. Leonard. 2013. "Richness of Human Gut Microbiome Correlates with Metabolic Markers." *Nature* 500, no. 7464, pp. 541–46. www.nature.com/nature/journal/v500/n7464/full/nature12506.html

Lee, H. 2012. "The Role of Local Food Availability in Explaining Obesity Risk among Young School-Aged Children." *Social Science & Medicine (1982)* 74, no. 8, pp. 1193–203. doi:10.1016/j.socscimed.2011.12.036

Liang, J., B.E. Matheson, W.H. Kaye, and K.N. Boutelle. 2014. "Neurocognitive Correlates of Obesity and Obesity-Related Behaviors in Children and Adolescents." *International Journal of Obesity (2005)* 38, no. 4, pp. 494–506. doi:10.1038/ijo.2013.142

Lioutas, E.D., and I. Tzimitra-Kalogianni. 2015. "'I Saw Santa Drinking Soda!' Advertising and Children's Food Preferences." *Child: Care, Health and Development* 41, no. 3, pp. 424–33. doi:10.1111/cch.12189

Llewellyn, A., M. Simmonds, C.G. Owen, and N. Woolacott. 2016. "Childhood Obesity as a Predictor of Morbidity in Adulthood: A Systematic Review and Meta-Analysis." *Obesity Reviews* 17, no. 1, pp. 56–67. doi:10.1111/obr.12316

Longhi, S., and G. Radetti. 2013. "Thyroid Function and Obesity." *Journal of Clinical Research in Pediatric Endocrinology* 5, no. 1, pp. 40–44. doi:10.4274/Jcrpe.856

Luhrmann, P.M., B. Edelmann-Schafer, and M. Neuhauser-Berthold. 2010. "Changes in Resting Metabolic Rate in an Elderly German Population: Cross-Sectional and Longitudinal Data." *The Journal of Nutrition, Health & Aging* 14, no. 3, pp. 232–36.

Lumeng, J.C., P. Forrest, D.P. Appugliese, N. Kaciroti, R.F. Corwyn, and R.H. Bradley. 2010. "Weight Status as a Predictor of Being Bullied in Third through Sixth Grades." *Pediatrics* 125, no. 6, pp. e1301–7. doi:10.1542/peds.2009-0774

Maloney, M.J., J.B. McGuire, and S.R. Daniels. 1988. "Reliability Testing of a Children's Version of the Eating Attitude Test." *Journal of the American Academy of Child & Adolescent Psychiatry* 27, no. 5, pp. 541–43. doi:10.1097/00004583-198809000-00004

Marcus, M.D., and M.A. Kalarchian. 2003. "Binge Eating in Children and Adolescents." *International Journal of Eating Disorders* 34, no. Sl, pp. S47–57. doi:10.1002/eat.10205

Mareno, N. 2014. "Parental Perception of Child Weight: A Concept Analysis." *Journal of Advanced Nursing* 70, no. 1, pp. 34–45. doi:10.1111/jan.12143

Markowitz, J.C., and M.M. Weissman. 2012. "Interpersonal Psychotherapy: Past, Present and Future." *Clinical Psychology & Psychotherapy* 19, no. 2, pp. 99–105. doi:10.1002/cpp.1774

Maximova, K., J.J. McGrath, T. Barnett, J. O'Loughlin, G. Paradis, and M. Lambert. 2008. "Do You See What I See? Weight Status Misperception and Exposure to Obesity among Children and Adolescents." *International Journal of Obesity (2005)* 32, no. 6, pp. 1008–15. doi:10.1038/ijo.2008.15

Mendelson, B.K., and D.R. White. 1985. "Development of Self-Body-Esteem in Overweight Youngsters." *Developmental Psychology* 21, no. 1, pp. 90–96. doi:10.1037/0012-1649.21.1.90

Miller, W.R., and S. Rollnick. 1991. *Motivational Interviewing: Preparing People for Change.* New York: Guilford Press.

Moore, L.C., C.V. Harris, and A.S. Bradlyn. 2012. "Exploring the Relationship Between Parental Concern and the Management of Childhood Obesity." *Maternal and Child Health Journal* 16, no. 4, pp. 902–8. doi:10.1007/s10995-011-0813-x

Müller, A.M., and S. Khoo. 2016. "Interdisciplinary, Child-Centred Collaboration Could Increase the Success of Potentially Successful Internet-Based Physical Activity Interventions." *Acta Paediatrica* 105, no. 3, pp. 234–43. doi:10.1111/apa.13307

National Institute of Justice. 2016. "Child Abuse and Maltreatment." www.nij.gov/topics/crime/child-abuse/pages/welcome.aspx#note1 (accessed April 1).

Neel, J.V. 1962. "Diabetes Mellitus: A 'Thrifty' Genotype Rendered Detrimental by 'Progress'?" *American Journal of Human Genetics* 14, no. 4, pp. 353–62.

Nguyen, V.T., D.E. Larson, R.K. Johnson, and M.I. Goran. 1996. "Fat Intake and Adiposity in Children of Lean and Obese Parents." *The American Journal of Clinical Nutrition* 63, no. 4, pp. 507–13.

Ogden, C.L., M.D. Carroll, B.K. Kit, and K.M. Flegal. 2014. "Prevalence of Childhood and Adult Obesity in the United States, 2011-2012." *JAMA* 311, no. 8, pp. 806–14. doi:10.1001/jama.2014.732

Oliver, S.R., J.S. Rosa, G.L. Milne, A.M. Pontello, H.L. Borntrager, S. Heydari, and P.R. Galassetti. 2010. "Increased Oxidative Stress and Altered Substrate Metabolism in Obese Children." *International Journal of Pediatric Obesity* 5, no. 5, pp. 436–44. doi:10.3109/17477160903545163

Olson, D.H. 2008. *FACES IV Manual.* Minneapolis, MN: Life Innovations.

O'Rahilly, S., and I.S. Farooqi. 2008. "Human Obesity: A Heritable Neurobehavioral Disorder That Is Highly Sensitive to Environmental Conditions." *Diabetes* 57, no. 11, pp. 2905–10. doi:10.2337/db08-0210

Parry, L.L., G. Netuveli, J. Parry, and S. Saxena. 2008. "A Systematic Review of Parental Perception of Overweight Status in Children." *The Journal of*

Ambulatory Care Management 31, no. 3, pp. 253–68. doi:10.1097/01. JAC.0000324671.29272.04

Pasch, L.A., C. Penilla, J.M. Tschann, S.M. Martinez, J. Deardorff, C.L. de Groat, S.E. Gregorich, E. Flores, N.F. Butte, and L.C. Greenspan. March 2016. "Preferred Child Body Size and Parental Underestimation of Child Weight in Mexican-American Families." *Maternal and Child Health Journal* 20, no. 9, pp. 1842–48. doi:10.1007/s10995-016-1987-z

Phillips, B.A., S. Gaudette, A. McCracken, S. Razzaq, K. Sutton, L. Speed, J. Thompson, and W. Ward. 2012. "Psychosocial Functioning in Children and Adolescents with Extreme Obesity." *Journal of Clinical Psychology in Medical Settings* 19, no. 3, pp. 277–84. doi:10.1007/s10880-011-9293-9

Phillips, K.L., L.A. Schieve, S. Visser, S. Boulet, A.J. Sharma, M.D. Kogan, C.A. Boyle, and M. Yeargin-Allsopp. 2014. "Prevalence and Impact of Unhealthy Weight in a National Sample of US Adolescents with Autism and Other Learning and Behavioral Disabilities." *Maternal and Child Health Journal* 18, no. 8, pp. 1964–75. doi:10.1007/s10995-014-1442-y

Piers, E.V., and D.S. Herzberg. 2002. *Piers-Harris 2: Piers-Harris Children's Self-Concept Scale.* Los Angeles, CA: Western Psychological Services.

Popkin, B.M., and J.R. Udry. 1998. "Adolescent Obesity Increases Significantly in Second and Third Generation U.S. Immigrants: The National Longitudinal Study of Adolescent Health." *The Journal of Nutrition* 128, no. 4, pp. 701–6.

Powell, L.M., and F.J. Chaloupka. 2009. "Food Prices and Obesity: Evidence and Policy Implications for Taxes and Subsidies." *Milbank Quarterly*, Obesity as a public policy issue, 87, no. 1, pp. 229–57. doi:10.1111/j.1468-0009.2009.00554.x

Price, K.L., M.E. Lee, G.A. Washington, and M.L. Brandt. 2015. "The Psychologist's Role in Ethical Decision Making: Adolescent Bariatric Surgery." *Clinical Practice in Pediatric Psychology*, Ethics and Pediatrics 3, no. 4, pp. 359–64. doi:10.1037/cpp0000117

Prochaska, J.O., W.F. Velicer, J.S. Rossi, M.G. Goldstein, B.H. Marcus, W. Rakowski, C. Fiore, L.L. Harlow, C.A. Redding, D. Rosenbloom, and S.R. Rossi. 1994. "Stages of Change and Decisional Balance for 12 Problem Behaviors." *Health Psychology* 13, no. 1, pp. 39–46. doi:10.1037/0278-6133.13.1.39

Puhl, R.M., and J.D. Latner. 2007. "Stigma, Obesity, and the Health of the Nation's Children." *Psychological Bulletin* 133, no. 4, pp. 557–80. doi:10.1037/0033-2909.133.4.557

Ramirez, A., K. Gallion, and C. Despres. 2014. "Latino Childhood Obesity." In *Obesity Interventions in Underserved Communities: Evidence and Directions*, eds. V.M. Brennan, S.K. Kumanyika, and R.E. Zambrana, 43–57. Baltimore, MD: Johns Hopkins University Press.

Reilly, J.J. 2010. "Assessment of Obesity in Children and Adolescents: Synthesis of Recent Systematic Reviews and Clinical Guidelines." *Journal of Human Nutrition and Dietetics* 23, no. 3, pp. 205–11. doi:10.1111/j.1365-277X.2010.01054.x

Reilly, J.J., J. Kelly, and D.C. Wilson. 2010. "Accuracy of Simple Clinical and Epidemiological Definitions of Childhood Obesity: Systematic Review and Evidence Appraisal." *Obesity Reviews: An Official Journal of the International Association for the Study of Obesity* 11, no. 9, pp. 645–55. doi:10.1111/j.1467-789X.2009.00709.x

Reyes, S., P. Peirano, P. Peigneux, B. Lozoff, and C. Algarin. 2015. "Inhibitory Control in Otherwise Healthy Overweight 10-Year-Old Children." *International Journal of Obesity (2005)* 39, no. 8, pp. 1230–35. doi:10.1038/ijo.2015.49

Robinson, L.E., and D.D. Wadsworth. 2010. "Stepping Toward Physical Activity Requirements: Integrating Pedometers into Early Childhood Settings." *Early Childhood Education Journal* 38, no. 2, pp. 95–102. doi:10.1007/s10643-010-0388-y

Ross, N., P.L. Yau, and A. Convit. October 2015. "Obesity, Fitness, and Brain Integrity in Adolescence." *Appetite* 93, pp. 44–50. doi:10.1016/j.appet.2015.03.033

Rotondi, M., P. Leporati, A. La Manna, B. Pirali, T. Mondello, R. Fonte, F. Magri, and L. Chiovato. 2009. "Raised Serum TSH Levels in Patients with Morbid Obesity: Is It Enough to Diagnose Subclinical Hypothyroidism?" *European Journal of Endocrinology/European Federation of Endocrine Societies* 160, no. 3, pp. 403–8. doi:10.1530/EJE-08-0734

Samadi, M., H. Sadrzade-Yeganeh, L. Azadbakht, K. Jafarian, A. Rahimi, and G. Sotoudeh. 2013. "Sensitivity and Specificity of Body Mass Index in Determining Obesity in Children." *Journal of Research in Medical Sciences: The Official Journal of Isfahan University of Medical Sciences* 18, no. 7, pp. 537–42.

Savage, J.S., J.O. Fisher, M. Marini, and L.L. Birch. 2012. "Serving Smaller Age-Appropriate Entree Portions to Children Aged 3–5 Y Increases Fruit and Vegetable Intake and Reduces Energy Density and Energy Intake at Lunch." *The American Journal of Clinical Nutrition* 95, no. 2, pp. 335–41. doi:10.3945/ajcn.111.017848

Shaikh, U., J. Nettiksimmons, and P. Romano. 2011. "Pediatric Obesity Management in Rural Clinics in California and the Role of Telehealth in Distance Education." *The Journal of Rural Health* 27, no. 3, pp. 263–69. doi:10.1111/j.1748-0361.2010.00335.x

Shapiro, J.R., S.L. Woolson, R.M. Hamer, M.A. Kalarchian, M.D. Marcus, and C.M. Bulik. 2007. "Evaluating Binge Eating Disorder in Children: Development of the Children's Binge Eating Disorder Scale (C-BEDS)."

International Journal of Eating Disorders 40, no. 1, pp. 82–89. doi:10.1002/eat.20318

Singh, G.K., M.D. Kogan, and P.C. van Dyck. 2008. "A Multilevel Analysis of State and Regional Disparities in Childhood and Adolescent Obesity in the United States." *Journal of Community Health: The Publication for Health Promotion and Disease Prevention* 33, no. 2, pp. 90–102. doi:10.1007/s10900-007-9071-7

Skinner, A.C., M. Weinberger, S. Mulvaney, D. Schlundt, and R.L. Rothman. 2008. "Accuracy of Perceptions of Overweight and Relation to Self-Care Behaviors among Adolescents with Type 2 Diabetes and Their Parents." *Diabetes Care* 31, no. 2, pp. 227–29. doi:10.2337/dc07-1214

Soechtig, S. 2014. *Fed Up.* United States: Atlas Films.

Story, M., N.E. Sherwood, J.H. Himes, M. Davis, D.R. Jacobs, Y. Cartwright, M. Smyth, and J. Rochon. 2003. "An After-School Obesity Prevention Program for African-American Girls: The Minnesota GEMS Pilot Study." *Ethnicity & Disease* 13, no. 1, pp. S54–64.

Straub, R.O. 2014. *Health Psychology: A Biopsychosocial Approach.* 4th ed. London: Worth Publishers.

Subar, A.F., V. Kipnis, R.P. Troiano, D. Midthune, D.A. Schoeller, S. Bingham, C.O. Sharbaugh, J. Trabulsi, S. Runswick, R. Ballard-Barbash, J. Sunshine, and A. Schatzkin. 2003. "Using Intake Biomarkers to Evaluate the Extent of Dietary Misreporting in a Large Sample of Adults: The OPEN Study." *American Journal of Epidemiology* 158, no. 1, pp. 1–13.

Suchert, V., R. Hanewinkel, and B. Isensee. July 2015. "Sedentary Behavior and Indicators of Mental Health in School-Aged Children and Adolescents: A Systematic Review." *Preventive Medicine: An International Journal Devoted to Practice and Theory* 76, pp. 48–57. doi:10.1016/j.ypmed.2015.03.026

Taylor, W.C., S.L. Upchurch, C.A. Brosnan, B.J. Selwyn, T.Q. Nguyen, E.T. Villagomez, and J.C. Meininger. 2014. "Features of the Built Environment Related to Physical Activity Friendliness and Children's Obesity and Other Risk Factors." *Public Health Nursing* 31, no. 6, pp. 545–55. doi:10.1111/phn.12144

ter Bogt, F.M. Tom, A.F.M. Saskia, V. Dorsselaer, K. Monshouwer, J.E.E. Verdurmen, R.C.M.E. Engels, and W.A.M. Vollebergh. 2006. "Body Mass Index and Body Weight Perception as Risk Factors for Internalizing and Externalizing Problem Behavior among Adolescents." *The Journal of Adolescent Health: Official Publication of the Society for Adolescent Medicine* 39, no. 1, pp. 27–34. doi:10.1016/j.jadohealth.2005.09.007

Tompkins, C.L., M. Seablom, and D.W. Brock. 2015. "Parental Perception of Child's Body Weight: A Systematic Review." *Journal of Child and Family Studies* 24, no. 5, pp. 1384–91. doi:10.1007/s10826-014-9945-0

Tovar, A., J.A. Emond, E. Hennessy, and D. Gilbert-Diamond. 2016. "An FTO Gene Variant Moderates the Association between Parental Restriction and Child BMI." *PloS One* 11, no. 5, p. e0155521. doi:10.1371/journal. pone.0155521

Tudor-Locke, C., R.P. Pangrazi, C.B. Corbin, W.J. Rutherford, S.D. Vincent, A. Raustorp, L.M. Tomson, and T.F. Cuddihy. 2004. "BMI-Referenced Standards for Recommended Pedometer-Determined Steps/day in Children." *Preventive Medicine* 38, no. 6, pp. 857–64. doi:10.1016/j.ypmed.2003.12.018

U.S. Department of Health and Human Services. 2010. "Healthy People 2020." www.healthypeople.gov/sites/default/files/HP2020_brochure_with_LHI_508_FNL.pdf

Valerio, G., V. Gallarato, O. D'Amico, M. Sticco, P. Tortorelli, E. Zito, R. Nugnes, E. Mozzillo, and A. Franzese. 2014. "Perceived Difficulty with Physical Tasks, Lifestyle, and Physical Performance in Obese Children." *BioMed Research International* 2014, pp. 1–7. doi:10.1155/2014/735764

Van Allen, J., K.B. Borner, L.A. Gayes, and R.G. Steele. 2015. "Weighing Physical Activity: The Impact of a Family-Based Group Lifestyle Intervention for Pediatric Obesity on Participants' Physical Activity." *Journal of Pediatric Psychology* 40, no. 2, pp. 193–202. doi:10.1093/jpepsy/jsu077

van Wijnen, L.G.C., P.R. Boluijt, H.B. Hoeven-Mulder, W.J.E. Bemelmans, and G.C. Wendel-Vos. 2010. "Weight Status, Psychological Health, Suicidal Thoughts, and Suicide Attempts in Dutch Adolescents: Results from the 2003 E-MOVO Project." *Obesity* 18, no. 5, pp. 1059–61. doi:10.1038/oby.2009.334

Vartanian, L.R. 2010. "'Obese People' vs 'Fat People': Impact of Group Label on Weight Bias." *Eating and Weight Disorders-Studies on Anorexia, Bulimia and Obesity* 15, no. 3, pp. 195–98. doi:10.1007/BF03325299

Vocks, S., B. Tuschen-Caffier, R. Pietrowsky, S.J. Rustenbach, A. Kersting, and S. Herpertz. 2010. "Meta-Analysis of the Effectiveness of Psychological and Pharmacological Treatments for Binge Eating Disorder." *International Journal of Eating Disorders* 43, no. 3, pp. 205–17.

Walley, A.J., A.I.F. Blakemore, and P. Froguel. October 2006. "Genetics of Obesity and the Prediction of Risk for Health." *Human Molecular Genetics* 15, no. 2, pp. R124–30. doi:10.1093/hmg/ddl215

Wang, S.S., K.D. Brownell, and T.A. Wadden. 2004. "The Influence of the Stigma of Obesity on Overweight Individuals." *International Journal of Obesity and Related Metabolic Disorders: Journal of the International Association for the Study of Obesity* 28, no. 10, pp. 1333–37. doi:10.1038/sj.ijo.0802730

Wang, Y.C., S.L. Gortmaker, and E.M. Taveras. 2011. "Trends and Racial/ethnic Disparities in Severe Obesity among US Children and Adolescents,

1976–2006." *International Journal of Pediatric Obesity* 6, no. 1, pp. 12–20. doi:10.3109/17477161003587774

Wardle, J., J. Waller, and E. Fox. 2002. "Age of Onset and Body Dissatisfaction in Obesity." *Addictive Behaviors* 27, no. 4, pp. 561–73.

Warin, M.J., and J.S. Gunson. 2013. "The Weight of the Word: Knowing Silences in Obesity Research." *Qualitative Health Research* 23, no. 12, pp. 1686–96. doi:10.1177/1049732313509894

Watts, A.W., C.Y. Lovato, S.I. Barr, R.M. Hanning, and L.C. Mâsse. December 2015. "A Qualitative Study Exploring How School and Community Environments Shape the Food Choices of Adolescents with Overweight/ obesity." *Appetite* 95, no. 2015, pp. 360–67. doi:10.1016/j.appet.2015.07.022

Webb, H.J., and M.J. Zimmer-Gembeck. 2015. "Body Image and Body Change Strategies within Friendship Dyads and Groups: Implications for Adolescent Appearance-based Rejection Sensitivity." *Social Development* 24, no. 1, pp. 1–19. doi:10.1111/sode.12081

Weis, R. 2014. *Introduction to Abnormal Child and Adolescent Psychology.* 2nd ed. Washington DC: Sage.

Weiss, D.L. 2013. *The Heavy.* New York: Ballantine Books.

White House Task Force on Childhood Obesity. 2010. "Solving the Problem of Childhood Obesity within a Generation." www.letsmove.gov/sites/letsmove. gov/files/TaskForce_on_Childhood_Obesity_May2010_FullReport.pdf

White, J., and R. Jago. 2012. "Prospective Associations between Physical Activity and Obesity among Adolescent Girls: Racial Differences and Implications for Prevention." *Archives of Pediatrics & Adolescent Medicine* 166, no. 6, pp. 522–27. doi:10.1001/archpediatrics.2012.99

Wilfley, D.E., M.A. Frank, R. Welch, E.B. Spurrell, and B.J. Rounsaville. 1998. "Adapting Interpersonal Psychotherapy to a Group Format (IPT-G) for Binge Eating Disorder: Toward a Model for Adapting Empirically Supported Treatments." *Psychotherapy Research* 8, no. 4, pp. 379–91. doi:10.1093/ptr/8.4.379

World Health Organization. 2016a. "Ending Childhood Obesity." http://apps. who.int/iris/bitstream/10665/204176/1/9789241510066_eng.pdf?ua=1

World Health Organization. 2016b. "Facts and Figures on Childhood Obesity." www.who.int/end-childhood-obesity/facts/en/

Yang, W., T. Kelly, and J. He. 2007. "Genetic Epidemiology of Obesity." *Epidemiologic Reviews* 29, no. 1, pp. 49–61. doi:10.1093/epirev/mxm004

Index

OTHER TITLES IN THIS CHILD CLINICAL PSYCHOLOGY "NUTS AND BOLTS" COLLECTION

Samuel T. Gontkovsky, *Editor*

Learning Disabilities
By Charles J. Golden, Lisa K. Lashley, Jared S. Link,
Matthew Zusman, Maya Pinjala, Christopher Tirado,
and Amber Deckard

Intellectual Disabilities
By Charles J. Golden, Lisa K. Lashley, Andrew Grego,
Johanna Messerly, Ronald Okolichany,
and Rachel Zachar

A Guide for Statistics in the Behavioral Sciences
By Jeff Foster

Momentum Press is one of the leading book publishers in the field of engineering, mathematics, health, and applied sciences. Momentum Press offers over 30 collections, including Aerospace, Biomedical, Civil, Environmental, Nanomaterials, Geotechnical, and many others.

Momentum Press is actively seeking collection editors as well as authors. For more information about becoming an MP author or collection editor, please visit
http://www.momentumpress.net/contact

Announcing Digital Content Crafted by Librarians

Momentum Press offers digital content as authoritative treatments of advanced engineering topics by leaders in their field. Hosted on ebrary, MP provides practitioners, researchers, faculty, and students in engineering, science, and industry with innovative electronic content in sensors and controls engineering, advanced energy engineering, manufacturing, and materials science.

Momentum Press offers library-friendly terms:

- perpetual access for a one-time fee
- no subscriptions or access fees required
- unlimited concurrent usage permitted
- downloadable PDFs provided
- free MARC records included
- free trials

The **Momentum Press** digital library is very affordable, with no obligation to buy in future years.

For more information, please visit **www.momentumpress.net/library** or to set up a trial in the US, please contact **mpsales@globalepress.com**.

CPSIA information can be obtained
at www.ICGtesting.com
Printed in the USA
FFOW03n1738030617
36344FF